Scams, ~~Hacking~~ & Cybersecurity

The Ultimate Guide to Online Safety and Privacy

May Brooks-Kempler

AUTHORITY PUBLISHING

Copyright © 2024 by May Brooks-Kempler

All rights reserved.

No portion of this book may be reproduced in any form without written permission from the publisher or author except as permitted by U.S. copyright law.

This book is intended to provide accurate and reliable information on the subject matter covered.

While every effort has been made to ensure the accuracy and completeness of the contents of this book, the publisher and author make no representations or warranties. They disclaim any implied warranties of merchantability or fitness for a particular purpose.

Neither the publisher nor the author shall be liable for any loss of profit or any other commercial damages, including but not limited to special, incidental, consequential, personal, or any other damages.

1st Edition 2024.

Contributing Author: Itamar Kempler

ISBN (Paperback): 978-1-965480-05-2

ISBN (eBook): 978-1-965480-04-5

Authority Publishing

www.authority-publishing.com

Printed in the United States of America.

To my mother who always believed in me, encouraged me and pushed me. I wish you were here to read this book.

To my Family - all I did, all I do is for you.

CONTENTS

Someone Moved My Data 01
A Few Facts to Get Us Started: 07
Introduction: 15
Basic Terminology 19
    What is Information Security? 19
        Confidentiality 21
        Integrity 22
        Availability 23
    The Differences Between Information Security and Cybersecurity 24
Common Threats: 27
    Malware 27
    Ransomware 28
        The History of Ransomware 29
        How Does a Computer Get Infected with Ransomware? 31
        Three Ways to Protect Yourself Against Ransomware Attacks: 32
        What Should You Do if You Get Hit by Ransomware? 33
        To Pay or Not to Pay? That is the Question. 35
Other Online Threats 37
The Threat of Social Engineering 47

Scams, Hacking, and Cybersecurity

Common Social Engineering Attacks:	52
Phishing, Examples and Warning Signs	52
The internet is like an elephant — it never forgets	69
Spear Phishing	70
Smishing, Examples and Warning Signs	74
Vishing	75
Consequences:	**79**
CIA Triad Violations	79
Confidentiality Violation	80
Data Integrity Failure	99
Failure of Data Availability	105
Risk Management	**125**
Practical Security Tools and Techniques	**131**
Awareness	132
Detecting Phishing Attacks	132
Detecting Vishing Attacks	134
General Awareness Tips	134
Using Encryption	135
A Brief History	136
Key Encryption Terminology	138
Encrypting Personal Data	140
Password Management	141
Password Threats	144
Choosing a Strong Password	145
How to Remember These Strong Passwords	147
Multi-Factor Authentication (MFA)	**152**

- **Safe Browsing** 155
  - Using Public Wi-Fi 159
- **Endpoint Security** 160
  - Security Updates 161
  - Mobile Device Security 164
- **Backups:** 166
  - What is the difference between backup and synchronization? 170
  - Keeping Physical Backup Media Safe 171
  - What About a Recovery Test? 172
- **Protecting our kids**[23] 176
  - The Dangers Children Face Online 178
  - Protecting Children Online: 182
  - Content Filtering: 183
  - Parental Monitoring and Control Tools 184
  - Setting Ground Rules: 185
- **What About Privacy?** 188
  - Privacy Settings 191

Predicting the Future 195
Glossary 199
References 203
Credits: 209

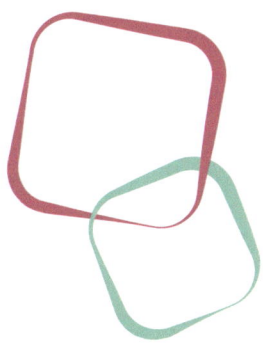

Someone Moved My Data

In the summer of 2019, I took my eldest daughter, who was ten years old at the time, on a trip to London. We travelled the streets, walked the parks, and visited the museums. While visiting the Science Museum, I suddenly noticed an old XT computer. Excited, I told her: "Shiri, this was my first computer!" "Mom," she replied, "you're ancient."

And if you think that was insulting, I wish you could have seen her face when I told her that Google and the internet didn't even exist when I was her age. It was a mixture of shock, pity, and admiration that I managed to survive my teenage years without Google.

Google was founded on September 4, 1998.

Scams, Hacking, and Cybersecurity

In the past two decades, someone moved our data.

Most people consider personal data as information on where we live, our ID number, bank accounts, marital status, etc. However, personal data includes so much more, for example - where we visited, where and when we plan to go on vacation, who our friends are, what basketball team we root for, whether we're job hunting, and so on.

In the past, all our data was stored in big binders in some dusty archives of insurance companies, healthcare service providers, and banks. After graduating high school, I interned at an insurance company in the summer of 2000, scanning thousands of documents. The company was digitizing its entire archive, an ambitious and uncommon project at the time.

Times have definitely changed. No one is using hard copies anymore. Try to remember: when was the last time you picked up a pen to write a letter or a document? As a child, my handwriting was a source of frustration. As one of my friends put it: "You have the handwriting of an old doctor who hates writing." No wonder I was a very early computer enthusiast.

Today our data is stored on various devices: smartphones, tablets, smartwatches, and of course, the cloud. Copies of every document we create are stored on multiple servers worldwide.

The term "Information Economy" was coined in the 1990s and refers to the growing emphasis on information technology and data-driven personalized services and experiences. Data today is treated as a currency. Users' data enables companies to provide customized experiences and services, and create targeted and effective marketing campaigns.

Scams, Hacking, and Cybersecurity

Our data has moved, and we're left asking some disturbing questions:

WHO KNOWS WHAT ABOUT ME?

WHAT IS CYBERSECURITY?

DOES PRIVACY STILL EXISTS?

HOW CAN I KEEP MY IMPORTANT DATA SAFE?

HOW TO MAINTAIN CYBERSECURITY?

Scams, Hacking, and Cybersecurity

I know our data has moved, and we have limited control over it. But be that as it may, I genuinely believe the internet is one of humanity's greatest and most important inventions, and it is here to stay, risks and all. The advantages of the internet outweigh the risks, and risks could be minimized by using the correct approaches and measures.

The data revolution is not the first technological revolution humanity has faced. If we jump into a time machine and travel back in time to the streets of London at the turn of the 20th century, we'll discover there weren't any pedestrian crossings. In fact, the UK introduced the first pedestrian crossings during the 1920s in selected areas, and the first set of standard traffic signal designs was published in 1937. Although none of us were born with the knowledge of how to cross a road safely, today, every parent teaches their child to look both ways before crossing the street.

I believe that just as parents teach their children road safety to help them navigate the world safely, internet safety is just as essential and should become a basic life skill that every parent should teach their kids.

As a cyber security professional, I see it as a personal mission to educate and give practical advice that will help people stay safe online. That's why I wrote this book.

In my 20 years in the data security field, I witnessed how technology changed and risks, and threats grew. Yet human use of the internet remained the same, I developed a set of tools and techniques that help keep myself, my clients and my loved ones, safe online, and in this book, I want to share those tools with you.

Scams, Hacking, and Cybersecurity

The book introduces basic data security concepts, continues to describe everyday data security scenarios and stories, and most importantly – suggests a simple set of tools and tips to improve your data security.

At the end of the book, you can find a glossary with all the terms mentioned in the book. The glossary can also be helpful as a reference to terms you might encounter elsewhere.

I consciously added interesting facts, stories, tools, and illustrations throughout the book to make the information clearer and relatable. I hope you will find the information in this book helpful, and that it will allow you to educate others on better internet security.

May Brooks-Kempler, June 2024

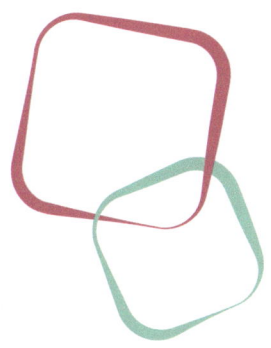

A Few Facts to Get Us Started:

On October 29, 1969, the first message was sent from a computer room at UCLA to a nearby lab at Menlo Park, the future site of Facebook headquarters. The message read 'LO.' It was supposed to read 'LOGIN,' but the communication was lost after the first two letters. It was the first message sent through the ARPANET network, the predecessor of the internet, which means that in 2019 the internet turned 50.

> **Cyber Fact**
>
> **?** In 2019, the total losses from ransomware attacks in the USA alone were estimated at over $1.3B. It is estimated that by the end of 2023, cyber breach cost will reach a staggering amount of 8$ trillion!

Scams, Hacking, and Cybersecurity

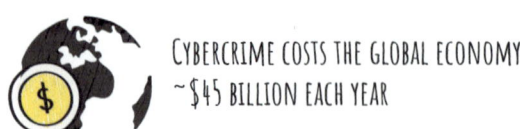 Cybercrime costs the global economy ~$45 billion each year

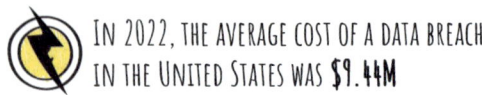 In 2022, the average cost of a data breach in the United States was $9.44M

 **95%** of all cyber incidents could have been prevented 22 billion records have been exposed in data breaches in 2022

 **17 BILLION RECORDS** have been exposed in data breaches in 2023

 **48%** of emails are spam and *phishing emails*

 The majority of cyber incidents occur due to human errors

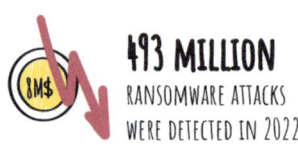 **493 MILLION** ransomware attacks were detected in 2022

 **1 IN EVERY 36** devices contain apps that are classified as malicious

One Small Step for Man, One Giant Leap for Mankind
(Neil Armstrong, July 1969)

The average smartphone we all carry in our pocket is more powerful than all the computers employed in the Apollo 11 moon landing put-together!

When we compare the computing power of the Apollo spacecraft with that of an average Smartphone, we consider three parameters: RAM, ROM, and processing power. Our smartphone is, first and foremost, a computer that also happens to make and receive phone calls.

But what do all these terms mean?

- RAM (Random Access Memory): A form of internal memory that can be read and changed in any order. The RAM holds the information of the applications installed on the device, your contacts list, and other data types. ROM (Read Only Memory): is the permanent memory of a computer. It cannot be electronically modified and retain the stored information even after the power is removed. This type of memory is also called non-volatile memory. This memory stores the operating system of a computer or a smartphone. The user cannot change the information stored in the ROM. The device manufacturer writes the data to the ROM during the manufacturing process, and it cannot be changed again, making this type of memory read-only.

- Processing power: determines how many tasks the computer can handle simultaneously. The available processing power depends on the type of processor, its frequency, and other parameters.

Scams, Hacking, and Cybersecurity

Apollo 11 vs. iPhone 11

RAM	32KB	4GB
ROM	72KB	512MB
Process Speed	0.043MHz	2490MHz

Scams, Hacking, and Cybersecurity

THIS AMAZING LITTLE DEVICE HOLDS 1,000 SONGS, AND IT GOES RIGHT IN MY POCKET
(STEVE JOBS, IPOD LAUNCH EVENT, OCTOBER 2001)

This quote is an excellent example of Steve Jobs' ability to explain complicated technical terms in a simple manner that anyone can understand. Instead of using technical terminology, Jobs described value and benefit in a way that users can understand: it holds 1,000 songs and fits in my pocket.

Back in 2008, I was working in one of the leading telecom companies in Israel. We received a 128MB USB flash drive as a gift, which back then cost over $100. In 2023, a flash drive with 128GB - 1,000 times the storage capacity – costs less than $20.

The cost of storage space keeps going down year after year. Today, the storage cost is no longer a significant factor when organizations develop their backup strategies.

Scams, Hacking, and Cybersecurity

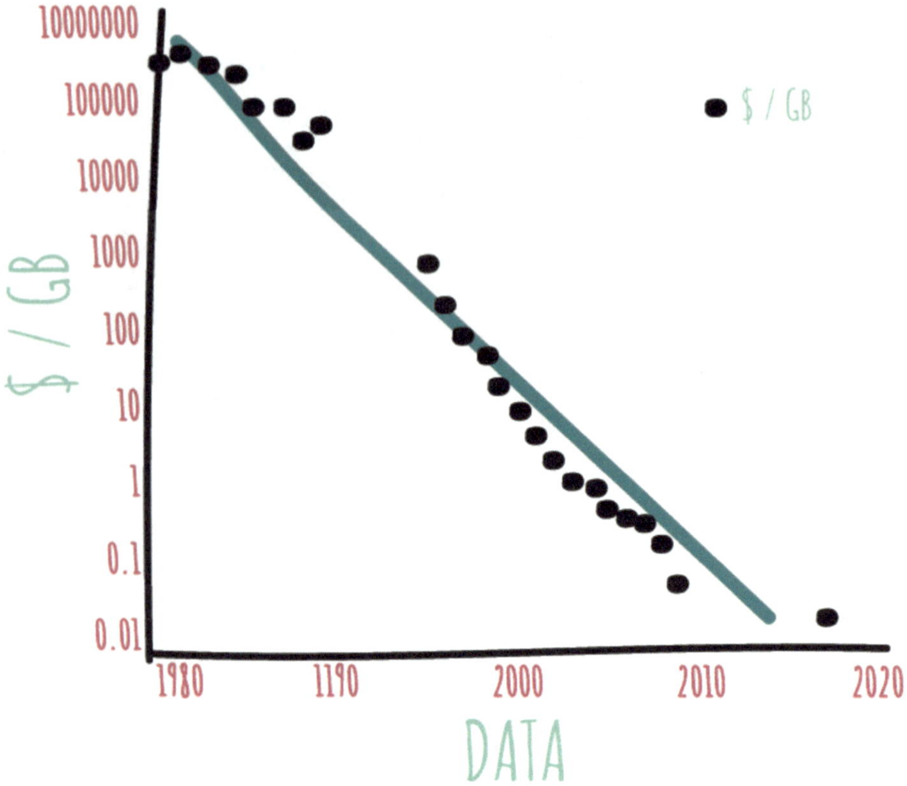

The way we create and store information has fundamentally changed. Long gone are the days in which taking a photo was a carefully planned and drawn-out process — lighting, composition, waiting until we shot an entire roll of film, and then waiting again for the film to be developed before we could see the result. Nowadays, we take dozens of photos virtually instantly. We upload and share memes, pictures, and songs, and the advent of cloud services has further increased the amount of data we hold.

However, the more information we have or others have about us, the greater the risks.

Scams, Hacking, and Cybersecurity

Data breaches, identity theft, ransomware attacks, extortion, and burglars using social media to know when the house is empty have become the new norm.

The most common cyber-attack types targeting individuals and organizations are:

1. Social Engineering (e.g. phishing)

2. Identity theft

3. Internet harassment and invasion of privacy

No one is immune to these attacks, and we should not take the threat lightly.

And this is why we're here, to minimize the risks by illuminating them and actively acting to protect our data while enjoying the wonderful things the internet has to offer.

Introduction:

I'm a technology enthusiast, gadget aficionado, addicted to the web, active on more social media platforms than I care to admit, and firmly believe that the internet is the greatest thing since sliced bread… probably even better.

I spend my days catching up on Facebook and Instagram, communicating via WhatsApp, and using about half a dozen email addresses every day.

Many people wonder how can someone who works in cyber security be so active online. The way I see it, the answer is simple. I know the benefits and dangers of using the web. I know my weak points, my vulnerabilities, and understand what needs to be done in order for me to stay safe online. After reading this book, you will also know how to do all of this.

A few years ago, I read an article that made me upset. Parents in a school formed a group to purchase "safe" mobile phones for their children. They had two reasons in mind:

Scams, Hacking, and Cybersecurity

1. To prevent their school-age children from getting addicted to a screen at a young age.

2. To protect their children from online dangers.

"We limit how much technology our kids use at home," said the late Steve Jobs in an interview for the New York Times in 2012. And he is not alone. Bill Gates expressed a similar sentiment as early as 2007.

I'm not a child psychologist, so I won't comment on the potential adverse effects of screen time. Like Jobs and Gates, I believe that every parent has to decide what is most appropriate and best for their child. With that said, I argue that we shouldn't discuss this subject in absolute terms. We shouldn't disallow children to use technology altogether and instead should promote better-educated use of technology.

I'm the first to admit the web could be a dangerous place. After all, I made a career of monitoring the risks and developing strategies and solutions to mitigate them. However, there are so many benefits to using the internet at young ages. My kids love podcasts; almost every family trip starts with choosing an episode for us to hear together. We listen to history stories, behind-the-music chapters, and economics for kids, when we went to France, we talked about Napoleon and when we visited Jerusalem, we went to see the wailing wall and talked about the six days war – not exactly part of the school curriculum.

Children do not reach a certain age and suddenly know how to start using the internet safely, all on their own. It's up to us to teach them good digital hygiene, just like we teach them how to brush their teeth (even if we're not dentists).

Scams, Hacking, and Cybersecurity

 Do we prevent children from using electricity because it's dangerous?

No. We teach them electrical safety from a young age[1].

I have three kids, all of whom were born into the digital age and all are heavy internet users.

I remember how when my eldest was 3-year-old she complained that "your phone is not as good as dad's." Back then, dad had a smartphone with a touchscreen, and I was still using my loyal Blackberry.

A lot has changed since then. I gave in, got a smartphone, and grown accustomed to having the world at my fingertips.

I can protest the use of smartphones all I want, but my children use their smartphones to listen to various educational podcasts, do their homework, communicate with friends and family around the world, and get access to information that they would not get in school.

What about the dangers? Do we know how to protect ourselves? Protect our children?

I believe that most people reading this book don't want to give up the internet altogether but would rather learn more about the risks and what they can do to remain safe online. Even experts can be affected by security breaches or online scams. I had my credit card stolen, albeit I don't know if it happened online. My parents-in-law fell victim to an Airbnb scam, and I constantly come across new and more sophisticated threats. However, I know how to review websites and messages, look for red flags,

---
[1] Thank you Oren Bratt for this example.

and these are the tools and strategies I want to share with you. "Give a man a fish and you feed him for a day; teach a man to fish and you feed him for a lifetime." Likewise, better online safety could be achieved only by sharing tools, knowledge, and strategies that will help us stay safe online.

The purpose of this book is not to discourage you from using the internet but to provide you with helpful information, strategies, and tips that will enable you to make the most out of this wonderful tool without taking unnecessary risks.

Basic Terminology

What is Information Security?

Two hundred years ago, highway robbers planning to rob a carriage carrying gold had to keep watch, learn the schedules and routes, or break into the bank looking for this information. In our digital era, criminals no longer need to physically break into a bank. Our data is online, and though protected, it is still vulnerable to malicious access and manipulation.

Another major difference is that in the 21st century, anyone — individuals, small businesses, or large corporations — has sensitive information that must be protected.

We live in a new world. A world in which our devices collect data about us, even when we're unaware of it. This data includes:

Scams, Hacking, and Cybersecurity

Our home and work address through applications such as Waze and Google Maps.

Who we had lunch with through location services and our online tags.

When we go to bed, because we put down the phone and stop using it for 6-7 hours.

Our hobbies by analyzing our search history, social media profiles, and our location.

Information security is the practice of protecting our data. Confidentiality, Integrity, and Availability form the CIA triad, a guiding concept at the heart of information security.

Scams, Hacking, and Cybersecurity

Confidentiality

Protecting sensitive information is a fundamental principle of information security, but not the only one. The two other fundamental principles of information security are **Integrity** and **Availability**.

> WHATEVER, IN THE COURSE OF MY PRACTICE,
> I MAY SEE OR HEAR (EVEN WHEN NOT INVITED),
> WHATEVER I MAY HAPPEN TO OBTAIN KNOWLEDGE OF,
> IF IT BE NOT PROPER TO REPEAT IT.
> (HIPPOCRATIC OATH)

2,500 years ago, Hippocrates II, considered the "Father of medicine," understood the importance of keeping patient information confidential. Patient-doctor confidentiality has been a fundamental tenet of medical ethics ever since.

We all have secrets; from the mundane credit card number and bank account details; through work-related, pricing tables, supplier agreements and customer contractors; and personal: medical conditions, hobbies, or sexual preferences.

How much would you be willing to pay to prevent an embarrassing or compromising video of yourself, from reaching your family, friends, and co-workers? This is not a hypothetical scenario. And I will cover online blackmail later in this book.

Scams, Hacking, and Cybersecurity

Integrity

When my husband and I bought our first house, we went to the bank to sign the mortgage documents to finalize the deal. The bank teller informed us that our bank account was foreclosed! I started to laugh awkwardly because I first thought it was a prank. Then I realized she was serious.

We started to investigate. Turns out, a local municipality had requested to foreclose our account due to an unpaid parking ticket. We used to live in a city where some streets were divided; one side of the road belongs to one local municipality, while the houses on the other side belong to a different municipality. I admit having received a couple of parking tickets because I didn't pay attention to which side of the street I parked on, but I always paid them and I didn't remember getting this ticket.

Do you know the saying, "When you ASSUME, you make an ASS out of U and ME"? Well, that was exactly what happened there.

The local municipality checked their records and sent the reminders to an address I hadn't lived in for more than three years at the time!

To add insult to injury, I didn't even own the car in question on the date the parking violation occurred. I sold it long before that.

If the local municipality had only checked the details with the DMV, they would have realized I no longer owned that car. And had the local municipality checked with the Ministry of the Interior, they would have known I moved and no longer live at that address.

This happened long ago, and since then things have improved a lot. Today the databases of most local municipalities are synced automatically with those of the various government offices so, at least in theory, they always have the most up-to-date data.

Scams, Hacking, and Cybersecurity

However, I hope this story demonstrates the importance of data integrity.

Healthcare is another field in which data integrity is essential. When an unconscious person arrives at the hospital, checking that person's medical records will provide the medical team with much-needed information such as blood type, medical history, medication history, and any known allergies. Out-of-date medical data could be far riskier than the inconvenience of a bank account foreclosure.

Availability

So far, I've described why Confidentiality and Integrity are essential. The third fundamental principle of information security is Availability.

As a technology enthusiast, I use several devices throughout the day: a laptop, a business tablet, and my smartphone. Furthermore, I'm a little obsessed with backing my data, which may or may not have something to do with the reputation I've earned in the family as someone who constantly breaks her phone. For these reasons, all my business data is stored in the cloud, not on my devices. It allows me flexibility. I don't have to worry about which device to take to a meeting; even if the device breaks, I still have access to all my data.

A few years ago, I was invited by a big telecommunication company to give a talk. I prepared a new presentation specific to this talk, arrived 15 minutes ahead, connected my tablet to the projector, and tried to connect to the internet.

There was no signal.

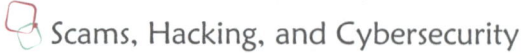 Scams, Hacking, and Cybersecurity

Never mind, I thought. I'll use my smartphone as a hotspot and download the presentation.

There was still no signal.

What was the problem, you ask?

Apparently, there was no cell reception in most areas of the building, nor reliable Wi-Fi! Talk about the cobbler having no shoes...

The clock was ticking, and I had already started to think how I would have to give my talk without the presentation.

I ended up going up two floors to an office area I knew had good cell reception and downloaded the presentation to my tablet. All's well that ends well.

I might have up-to-date and accurate data (integrity) that I keep well secured (confidentiality), but it's only useful to me if it's unavailable when I need it. This is exactly the point when discussing data availability.

By the way, after that ordeal, I started taking a flash drive with the presentation on it with me, just in case.

The Differences Between Information Security and Cybersecurity

Is there a difference between information security and Cybersecurity?

Yes! It's a whole other title!

Jokes aside, there are important distinctions between the two. We have already learned that information security is all about the Confidentiality, Integrity, and Availability of the **data**. What is Cybersecurity, then?

The term Cyber is short for Cybernetics and refers to telecommunication infrastructure. Any device connected to a network, including the internet, is part of cyberspace — the intersection between hardware, software, and humans.

Consider traffic lights. The information about the traffic light signal timing isn't very valuable in itself. However, compromising the traffic management infrastructure — or worse, taking it down — could have local and even national consequences. Imagine the chaos if all traffic lights on a major arterial road suddenly stop working. Now try to imagine the chaos on a city and country-wide scale!

Cybersecurity is the protection of national and other critical infrastructures. Yet, it is typically transparent to the average user. Indeed, an attack on the cyberinfrastructure in your area will disrupt your day and cause inconvenience, but you can't do much on your own to improve infrastructures' cybersecurity.

Therefore, this book focuses on Information Security because it has a bigger role and impact on our everyday lives.

While the media and many professionals often use the terms *information security* and *cybersecurity* interchangeably, it's important to note that there are important distinctions between them.

Information security is all about the information itself, whether it's stored on hard drives or hard copies, and cybersecurity is all about the protection of the interconnected cyber realm. It's not just the information, it's the data and innerworkings of it.

Common Threats:

Now it's time to distinguish between various threats we should all be aware of:

Malware

Malware is malicious code designed to damage computers, servers, or embedded systems[2]. Common malware variants include computer viruses, spyware, Trojan horses, and ransomware

Different malware variants are designed to cause different types of damage.

Spyware is used to gather information by logging the user activity on the device.

---

[2] An embedded system is any device with a dedicated combination of computer hardware and software designed to perform a specific function. For example: elevators, medical devices, irrigation systems, and even the Robot vacuum many have at home.

Scams, Hacking, and Cybersecurity

Trojan Horse is a malware that is aimed at gaining unauthorized access to sensitive, confidential, and guarded information stored on a device.

Computer Viruses can perform various harmful activities, including opening or closing files, changing computer settings, and even destroying the data stored on a hard drive.

Ransomware

In the past, criminals who wanted to extort money would kidnap people for ransom. Kidnapping, however, requires a great deal of planning and is very risky: from choosing the target, through the logistics of the abduction and negotiation, to the risk of the victim learning something about the kidnappers' identity while imprisoned.

Cybercriminals of the 21st century took the concept of kidnapping and perfected it. Instead of kidnapping a person, they hijack information. Because nearly all businesses depend on computer systems to run their business, virtually all businesses (and anyone who uses a computer, for that matter) are a target.

Ransomware is a malicious computer program that encrypts all the user files on the computer, thus making them inaccessible, and then demands a ransom payment to decrypt them.

Ransomware attacks have become widespread and commonplace, and today can be executed even without special or advanced technical skills. Cybercriminals offer Ransomware-as-a-Service (RAAS) through the Darknet, a business model allowing even a novice cybercriminal to execute a ransomware attack without difficulty in exchange for sharing the ransom money.

It's a business model, and an entire industry has been built around ransomware. Independent hackers, criminal organizations, and sometimes even governments dedicate a lot of resources to the distribution and execution of ransomware attacks. For example, some ransomware variants provide a 'Helpline' that victims can call for help if they don't understand how to pay the ransom or use the decryption key.

Believe it or not, cybercriminals are concerned with maintaining a reputation. If a certain ransomware attack group gains a reputation for not being trustworthy, in other words, not providing the decryption key after the ransom is paid, victims will be less likely to pay the ransom, thus defeating the purpose of a ransomware attack in the first place

They might be thieves, but they have honor, and they will guide the victims to decrypt their data once the ransom is paid.

The History of Ransomware

In 1989, Joseph L Popp, a Harvard graduate anthropologist, attended a conference for AIDS researchers. At the conference, Joseph handed out floppy disks of seemingly freeware computer programs for analyzing AIDS research data. However, Joseph also included a hidden program that counted the number of times the computer was booted. When the boot count reached 90 reboots, the dormant program was activated[3], it encrypted the data stored on the computer, and displayed the following message:

---

[3] This dormant program type is called a logical bomb or time bomb. It is a malicious program, aka malware, that is activated when specific conditions are met, e.g., several system reboots, a specific date is reached, a specific amount of time has passed since infection, etc. Logical bombs are tricky to identify.

Scams, Hacking, and Cybersecurity

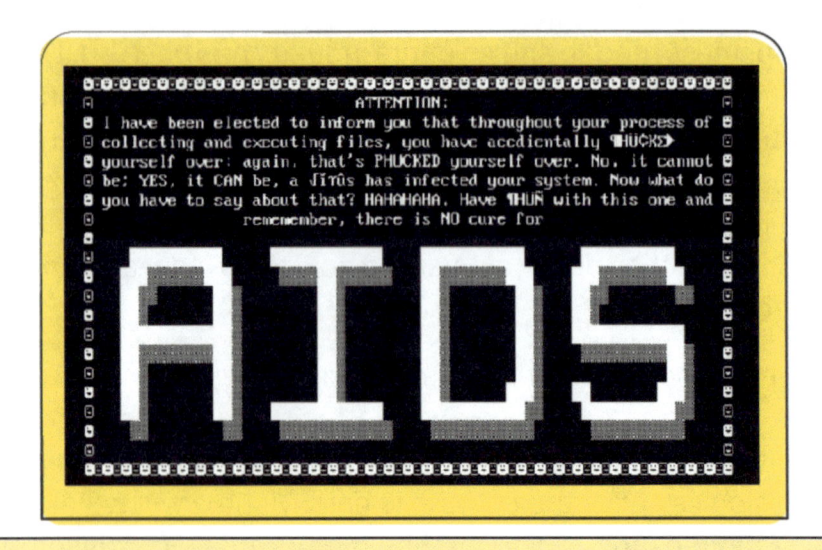

```
ATTENTION:
I have been elected to inform you that throughout your process of
collecting and executing files, you have accidentally $HUCK$>
yourself over; again, that's PHUCKED yourself over. No, it cannot
be; YES, it CAN be, a Virus has infected your system. Now what do
you have to say about that? HAHAHAHA. Have THUN with this one and
              remember, there is NO cure for

                          AIDS
```

The victims were asked to transfer $189 to a bank account in Panama in exchange for the decryption key that would allow them to restore their data.

Joseph, a member of the Flying Doctors movement, was identified as the program's author. He defended his actions by arguing that he donated the ransom money for the purpose of furthering AIDS research.

Joseph was arrested in the UK but was never prosecuted because he was declared mentally unfit to stand trial and was repatriated to the USA.

The AIDS ransomware is the first ransomware attack in history.

Between 1989-2005 there were no reports regarding large-scale ransomware attacks; in fact, up until 2013 such attacks were very rare. However, since the CryptoLocker ransomware attack in 2013, ransomware attacks have been on the rise and are considered one of the most significant current cyber threats.

Scams, Hacking, and Cybersecurity

Ransomware Timeline

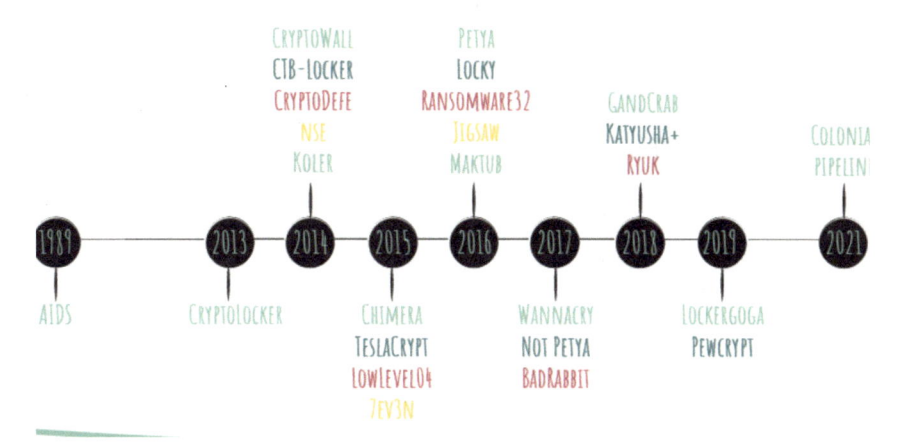

1989		AIDS
2013		CRYPTOLOCKER
2014	CRYPTOWALL, CTB-LOCKER, CRYPTODEFE, NSE, KOLER	
2015		CHIMERA, TESLACRYPT, LOWLEVEL04, 7EV3N
2016	PETYA, LOCKY, RANSOMWARE32, JIGSAW, MAKTUB	
2017		WANNACRY, NOT PETYA, BADRABBIT
2018	GANDCRAB, KATYUSHA+, RYUK	
2019		LOCKERGOGA, PEWCRYPT
2021	COLONIA PIPELIN	

Recently, we've witnessed some large-scale ransomware attacks, the consequences of which affected most of the world. I'll cover specific examples later in this book.

How Does a Computer Get Infected with Ransomware?

Usually, computers get infected with ransomware due to user errors: clicking on a malicious link on an email, downloading and running a file, plugging a flash drive from an unknown source, or clicking on an advertisement on some random website.

In The Threat of Social Engineering chapter, you will learn how to efficiently identify Phishing attacks[4], which are one of the primary methods for delivering a ransomware attack. Every time you save or open a file you've received from an unknown and untrustworthy source; you expose yourself to this type of risk.

---

[4] A social engineering attack is designed to trick the user into revealing sensitive information to the attacker or to downloading malicious software.

Scams, Hacking, and Cybersecurity

Three Ways to Protect Yourself Against Ransomware Attacks:

- **Awareness:** first and foremost, this book aims to raise cybersecurity awareness. Being aware will help you identify risks and avoid them. This book allows you to develop your very own "Spidey Sense" for different types of cyber-attacks. Infecting a device with ransomware usually requires user involvement in clicking a link or executing a file. So, in this case, it is totally up to us to look for warning signs like – an unknown sender, non-personal greeting, unexpected correspondence, use of manipulation in a message, and other warning signs we'll cover later. This is only the beginning of this guide, and you don't have all the knowledge yet, but even now, you can protect yourself by being a little less trusting, and if you see a message that seems too good to be true, remember it probably is. As you continue your journey with this book, you'll notice that your Spidey senses are getting sharper, however, there are two technological tools you can implement today that will help you protect yourself against the impact of a ransomware attack.

- **Backup:** in a perfect world, ransomware wouldn't exist. However, in our world, we want to minimize its potential disruption to our lives. The easiest way to achieve this goal is to back up your data so that even if you fall victim to a ransomware attack, or just drop a cup of coffee on your laptop, your loss would be minimal. I strongly recommend backing up data, or at least your most important data, to the cloud and an external storage device. In the Backups chapter, you'll find useful tips on how to set up your backup.

    When I was writing this book, I used several devices: a laptop, a tablet, and sometimes even my smartphone for quick edits and comments. Thus, I created a shared folder on the cloud where I kept the manuscript and all other related materials. Moreover, I emailed myself the most recent manuscript version after each writing session. Once every couple of weeks, I also routinely back up all my important folders to an external storage device. Seems a bit much? Perhaps, but better safe than sorry. It's important to add that some ransomwares are triggered after a specific time period (aka - timebomb), meaning that a backup copy of the data may also be infected with the ransomware, so even a backup cannot keep you 100% safe.

- **Security updates:** Using an outdated operating system or anti-virus software is equivalent to taking the 2019 flu vaccination against covid-19, it just doesn't work. Against the current threats you must use the current protection tools. Applying the latest updates to your operating system and security software will enable it to identify and block various threats, including certain ransomware attacks. At home, we are responsible for keeping our devices up to date. Read more in the Backups chapter.

What Should You Do if You Get Hit by Ransomware?

Unfortunately, despite security professionals' best efforts and the growing awareness of the subject worldwide, ransomware attacks are still very effective. And for someone who gets hit by ransomware, the first question is always: to pay or not to pay?

The following flow chart describes the thought process when deciding whether or not to pay the ransom.

Scams, Hacking, and Cybersecurity

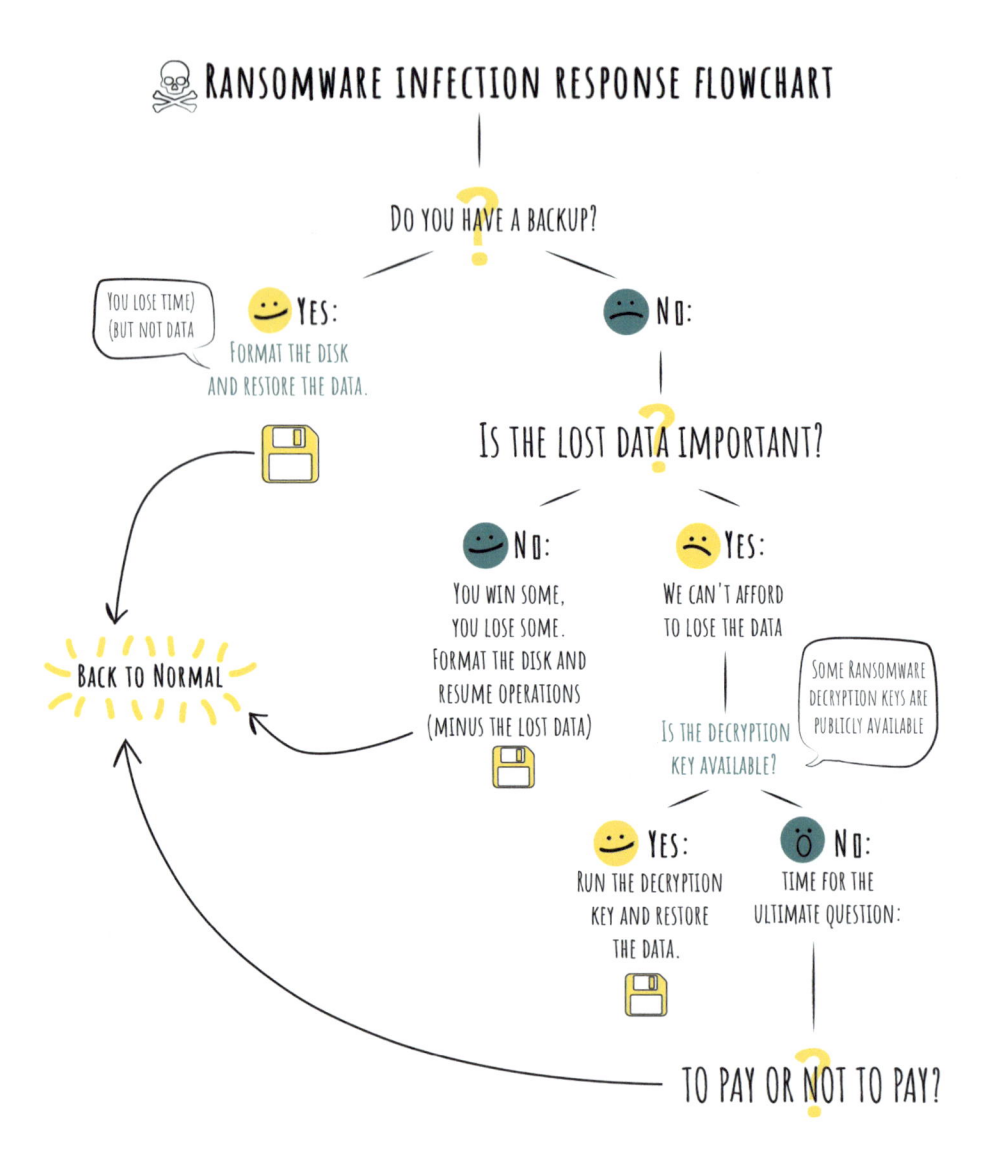

☠ Ransomware infection response flowchart

Do you have a backup? ❓

— **Yes:** Format the disk and restore the data.
   (You lose time, but not data) → **Back to Normal** 💾

— **No:**

  Is the lost data important? ❓

  — **No:** You win some, you lose some. Format the disk and resume operations (minus the lost data) → **Back to Normal** 💾

  — **Yes:** We can't afford to lose the data.

    Is the decryption key available?
    (Some ransomware decryption keys are publicly available)

    — **Yes:** Run the decryption key and restore the data. → **Back to Normal** 💾

    — **No:** Time for the ultimate question:

      TO PAY OR NOT TO PAY? ❓ → **Back to Normal**

To Pay or Not to Pay? That is the Question.

If your computer is infected by ransomware and you do not have an updated backup, there are only two options:

1. Accept the data is lost

2. Pay the ransom

Assuming the first option is out of the question because the information is mission-critical, there's one question left:

Should I negotiate with criminals?

There is no one-size-fits-all answer. Many people who chose to pay the ransom did receive the decryption key because, as I already mentioned, the criminals want to establish a reputation for being true to their word. Otherwise, no one will even consider paying the ransom.

However, there are many reported cases where people paid the ransom but never got the decryption key. Furthermore, some ransomware attacks are more targeted and specific than others, resulting in very different ransom sum requests sent to private individuals vs. businesses.

The decision of whether to pay the ransom or not should weigh the value of the lost data against the ransom amount.

On the morning of my mother's funeral, I was looking for pictures of us from a trip we went on together. My main computer didn't work at the time, and for whatever reason, when I tried to access my external storage device, it took a while before the disk content showed up. During those moments, I was willing to pay anything for those pictures.

Scams, Hacking, and Cybersecurity

So no judgment here if someone decides to pay the ransom in order to retrieve valuable data but let's be honest: It's much easier to properly back up the data.

Another aspect to consider is that as long as people keep paying the ransom, cybercriminals will be incentivized to continue with ransomware attacks. The No More Ransom Project (nomoreransom.org) was founded to raise public awareness of ransomware attacks and help ransomware victims retrieve their encrypted data without paying the ransom, thus making ransomware attacks less financially lucrative for criminals. The project is a joint initiative of European law enforcement agencies (Europol, Netherlands police) and cybersecurity companies (Kaspersky, McAfee)

Other Online Threats

Since we all use the internet, we are all vulnerable to some degree.

It's time to introduce some of the threat actors:

- Hackers: Skilled computer experts who can break into computer systems through the network and access data that would otherwise be unavailable to them. The art of Hacking can be used for good or bad. Hackers use malwares such as Trojan horses, computer viruses, and worms, to harm their potential targets.

Not all Hackers are born equal. There are levels to their skills and abilities. Most professional hackers have started as what the community calls Script Kiddies, unskilled individuals who use existing scripts or programs. Script Kiddies are typically curious and very intelligent teenagers. Their first targets often include their school's computer systems or the companies where their parents work, as they assume it won't get them into too much trouble for it. They usually cause little to moderate harm. They learn hacking by watching YouTube videos and playing around with free tools that they find on the web. Some will take a real interest in the field and learn how to write short pieces of code (scripts) of their own and how computer networks and systems work. At some point, an individual like that can stop being a simple Script Kiddie and develop their own tools and attacks – venturing as a professional hacker – either doing bad and hurting organizations and individuals (black hat hacker) or doing good and protecting the internet (white hat hacker).

Hackers are typically very intelligent, like to work alone, and tend to dig deep into subjects they find interesting.

There are two types of hacking attacks:

- Random attack: a broad attack that is not targeting a particular individual or organization. Most phishing attacks falls under this category because they aim to infect as many computer systems as possible and not target a specific individual or organization. These attacks could cause severe damage, but because they cast a very wide net, it is easier for cybersecurity companies to identify the threat and update their software to block it.

- Targeted attack: an attack where the attackers actively pursue a specific individual or organization[5]. The good news is that most of us are not interesting enough for hackers to bother targeting specifically. On the other hand, if a hacker does target us, we're in serious trouble. Targeted attacks are usually sophisticated and persistent. It will take time for Cybersecurity companies to identify a targeted cyber event if they identify it at all. There are also different levels

---

[5] Keep in mind that while you personally may not be THAT interesting, your company may very well be. Hackers always find the path of least resistance.

of targeted attacks. There is a difference between a very determined teenager who might spend days and maybe even several weeks , and a country-sponsored threat actor who targets national infrastructure systems, such as the electrical grid or water supply networks and can work on it for months or even years.

- Hacktivism: hackers are largely thought of as anarchists who seek to promote chaos. While some hackers fit that description, this is far from being the entire story. As I've mentioned, hackers are very intelligent and often have a clear agenda. Hacktivism is any form of hacking designed to promote ideological causes.

    One of the major Hacktivist movements is Anonymous. Anonymous members disguise themselves on videos by wearing Guy Fawkes masks.[6]

---

[6] Guy Fawkes was an English Catholic soldier, involved in the plot to assassinate King James in 1605. He was caught and executed. To this day, some commonwealth countries celebrate Guy Fawkes Night with bonfires, fireworks display, and burning Guy Fawkes effigies.

Scams, Hacking, and Cybersecurity

Anonymous was involved in attacks against various targets, including the U.S. government, the government of Israel, the Church of Scientology, various banks in Cyprus, NASA, Thai prisons, and the Ku Klux Klan (KKK) website.

The group members use private forums on the web and the Darknet to suggest new targets.

> *The Darknet is a hidden network on the internet that is not accessible through regular search engines and can only be accessed using an anonymized browser like Tor. The Darknet is popular among hackers because it allows them to communicate anonymously.*

Since a successful cyber-attack, especially an attack targeting large organizations, requires many individual attackers to work together in unison, the group publishes a target list before launching an attack campaign.

These coordinated attacks are called Op, short for operation, followed by the target (Israel, KKK, and so on):

* #OpISRAEL: Since 2013, Anonymous has launched an annual coordinated cyber-attack against Israeli government and private websites to disrupt traffic and take them down. In the weeks leading to the attack, lists of websites expected to be targeted are published in online forums. In #OpIsrael websites are targeted only because they are Israeli, so when I created my first blog, I consciously selected a .com domain even though the website was for an Israeli audience. I wanted to reduce the risk of my website appearing on one of those targeted website lists.

The chances that my blog would have ended up in one of those lists were rather slim, but I decided this was one risk I could live without.

Anonymous doesn't focus on Israel alone. The group attacks a wide variety of targets based on all kinds of ideologies and agendas. For example:

* #OpKKK: in 2005, Anonymous revealed the names of active members of the white supremacist hate group the Ku Klux Klan (KKK)

* #OpPARIS: in November 2015, a series of coordinated terrorist attacks occurred in Paris, resulting in 130 fatalities. A few days after the attack, Anonymous launched a coordinated cyber-attack against ISIS websites and computer systems. After Anonymous announced its plan, ISIS responded by saying they were not worried and that Anonymous was welcome to try. A couple of days after, Anonymous took down more than 5,000 Twitter accounts associated with the terror organization. However, the list of accounts published by Anonymous also included legitimate accounts, including those of U.S. President Barak Obama, Hillary Clinton, and the BBC News.

Anonymous is known for its heavy use of propaganda techniques, such as videos and posts on social media intended to increase support for their causes and create fear as part of the psychological warfare.

An example of one of Anonymous' propaganda videos is a video[7] posted to the official Anonymous YouTube channel after the deadly November 2015 Paris terror attacks, in which

---

[7] https://www.youtube.com/watch?v=5UjIqwf9fyk

Scams, Hacking, and Cybersecurity

the Hacktivist group announced they would be tracking the terror groups responsively for those attacks.

[QR code]

While Anonymous gets a lot of attention, they are far from being the only Hacktivism group. There are many other Hacktivism groups, each with its own agendas.

An interesting example is the Ashley Madison[8] data breach in 2015. Ashley Madison is a dating website, but unlike traditional online dating websites designed for single people, Ashely Madison used the slogan "Life is short. Have an affair" encouraging individuals to have extramarital affairs. On July 2015, a group self-proclaimed 'The Impact Team' breached Ashely Madison's website and stole user data. The group then contacted Ashely Madison's management and threatened that if they did not shut down the website, the group would expose Ashley Madison's users' identities. They immediately published details that were supposed to be encrypted for paying customers, causing embarrassment to the website operator.

Obviously, Ashley Madison's executives were not thrilled with the prospect of losing their golden goose; thus, they negotiated with the attackers and paid them a heavy ransom to leave the database alone. However, they did not consider

---

[8] Checkout "Ashley Madison: Sex, Lies & Scandal" released by Netflix in 2024

the real motivation behind the attack. The attackers were probably very happy to receive the money, but they still leaked the database since their objective was to close the website as they deemed it immoral.

This cyber-attack had tragic consequences. Reports soon followed about two men, a pastor from New Orleans and a Policeman from San Antonio, who took their own lives citing, the leak as the reason.

The exposure of the Ashely Madison database also led to some politicians withdrawing their candidacies after being linked to the scandal.

The Ashely Madison data breach is not very interesting from a technical perceptive. The more interesting question is, in my opinion, whether Hacktivism will become a tool for activists from all corners of the political and social spectrum. Will ubiquitous access to hacking tools likely lead to more cyber-attacks over pollical and social agendas? Such as targeting meat product manufacturers by vegan Hacktivism groups, pharmaceutical companies by anti-vaxxers, or energy companies by environmental activists.

During global events such as the Covid-19 pandemic, the US presidential election, the Russia-Ukraine War, and the Israel-Hamas conflict, we've seen heavy usage of social media and Hacktivism techniques all aimed at influencing public opinion.

Knowledge is Power

Will Hacktivism become an instrument used to influence decision making, Will hackers collect data on judges, government officials, and head of states for the purpose of extortion or to politically manipulate them?

Perhaps it's already happening?

I can't answer this question, but Hacktivism is definitely an interesting trend that I'm following closely.

> I KNOW NOT WITH WHAT WEAPONS WORLD WAR III WILL BE FOUGHT, BUT WORLD WAR IV WILL BE FOUGHT WITH STICKS AND STONES
> (ALBERT EINSTEIN)

Cyberwarfare

- Consider these two timelines:
  * In 1981, Iraq was building its nuclear program. The Israeli government launched a surprise airstrike, Operation Opera, in which a squadron of eight Israeli Air Force fighter jets bombed and destroyed the Iraq nuclear reactor. Among the jet fighter pilots was the late Col. Ilan Ramon, who later became the first Israeli Astronaut and was killed in the fatal re-entry accident of the Columbia space shuttle in 2003.
  * Two years later, in 1983, the movie WarGames was released. The plot follows David, a young hacker portrayed by Matthew Broderick, who while trying to hack a computer game company in search of new video games, breaks into a supercomputer called War Operation Plan Response (WOPR) and briefly ran a simulation that convinced

military personnel that actual Soviet nuclear missiles were inbound, thus almost starting World War III

These two seemingly unrelated timelines converged in 2010 when the Stuxnet malware was uncovered in Irani nuclear facilities. Stuxnet infected computers that control devices involved in the uranium enrichment in Iran's nuclear facilities. The malware affected the rotational speed control of the centrifuges, changing the speed periodically until the excessive vibrations caused by the change in speed eventually destroyed the centrifuges. Stuxnet is claimed to have destroyed over 20% of nuclear centrifuges in the Iranian Nuclear Program. Stuxnet is a highly sophisticated malware. It's also very costly. The malware exploited an unprecedented number of zero-day vulnerabilities (a flaw in software or hardware the vendor has yet to learn about), each going quickly for more than $100,000 on the Darknet. The malware spread through the network, looking for specific parameters and systems used in an Iranian nuclear facility. Once the malware detects it is in the right place, it delivers the payload. The malware also tricked the nuclear facility control systems into thinking operation speeds remained normal, thus not giving supervisors any cause for suspicion until it was too late. Analysis on the target, the level of sophistication of the malware, and code snippets that included quotes from the bible led Iran, and the world media to claim Stuxnet was the work of Israel and the USA; specifically unit 8200 and the NSA. Israel and the USA never confirmed that they created Stuxnet, but these days the common belief is that they are behind the cyberattacks on Iranian nuclear facilities.

Throughout the years, many cyber-attacks have been attributed to Iran, Israel, USA, Russia, Ukraine, China etc.

Scams, Hacking, and Cybersecurity

These events demonstrate that cyber warfare is not some Hollywood sci-fi, it's the new reality. Stuxnet proved that reality surpasses imagination, and that James Bond was replaced by Q.

The Threat of Social Engineering

Did you know you're an engineer? Social engineering is the art of manipulation, i.e., the ability to get people to perform actions or divulge confidential information.

'Last one in the car is a rotten egg'! If you swing by our house on school days you might hear this cry at around 7AM. I want to get to work on time, and my kids want to watch TV, so I use psychology to motivate and urge them in a way that achieves the desired outcome. In this case, I turn to their competitiveness; this is what a social engineer does. Social engineering uses human emotions to motivate and influence people to advance the manipulators' interests. We are all social engineers.

Scams, Hacking, and Cybersecurity

What emotions can motivate us to act?

- **Fear:** Fear is a great motivator. Phishing attacks often impersonate security messages from known and trusted services. For example: a message notifying the user their PayPal account was suspended due to suspicious activity. The fear of losing personal data or the account getting suspended motivates us to click on links that otherwise might have raised our suspicion.s

- **Urgency:** This is another great motivator. It is no coincidence that phishing attacks often use both fear and urgency because they supplement each other. For example, a phishing message about a suspicious activity on the user's Facebook account, followed by a warning that if the account is not verified within 24 hours, it will be permanently closed.

- **Greed:** People like bargains and discounts. Even the wealthiest person in the world likes a good bargain. Cybercriminals use greed to motivate people into action. A special discount, a limited time offer (combining greed and urgency), and the chance to earn a handsome commission by assisting a Nigerian prince in claiming his fortune are all techniques cyber criminals implement to urge people to click on a link or divulge information by typing them into a form.

- **Curiosity:** People love secrets, even more so, they love other people's secrets. Who wouldn't click on an attached file that was seemingly sent by the HR department and is titled 'Management Salary List'? In the past, criminals used to hand out CDs of seemingly legitimate software at conferences and trade shows. Today, phishing attacks are delivered through email, but the basic principle is the same.

Scams, Hacking, and Cybersecurity

FEAR

"I know what you did, I'll tell everyone"

GREED

"I WON!"
SALE! SPECIAL OFFER

The emotions that triggers us

URGENCY

"Click now, or…"
TODAY ONLY!

CURIOSITY

CONFIDENTIAL
TOP SECRET

Scams, Hacking, and Cybersecurity

By the way, if these techniques seem familiar to you from marketing campaigns – you're absolutely right! Social engineering is used all the time in the marketing world to get us to buy something NOW. Just try and book a hotel online and see how they "only have 1 room left," then change your search for two rooms, and lo and behold – it's your lucky day! Now they have two rooms left. So, be aware of these manipulations; yes, sometimes it's the last room, but sometimes it's just a way to get you to commit.

The story of the Gentleman Thief

> One morning, Mike got up, got dressed, made a sandwich for lunch, filled his travel mug with coffee, and locked the door behind him as he left for the office. "Strange", he thought, "I could have sworn that I parked the car here last night". A few moments later, he realized his car had been stolen. Instead of a regular day at the office, Mike spent the day filing a police report, and calling the insurance company, all while trying to get some work done over the phone. Around noon, he received a call from his wife, Nancy. She found the car parked next to the house, with a note that began with an apology. It was left there by the thief. The thief apologized for taking the car and said he had only borrowed it due to an emergency. As an apology, the thief booked a reservation in a nice restaurant for Mike and Nancy to go to dinner. When Nancy called the restaurant, they confirmed that a reservation had been made for that evening and that the meal was already paid for. Mike withdrew the police complaint he had filed earlier that day, and the insurance claim, and later in the evening, he and Nancy went out to dinner. The restaurant had a vibrant atmosphere and excellent food, and Mike and Nancy had a great evening. Nothing, however, prepared them for what came next.

When they returned home, they found a handwritten note on the door. It was from the car thief, asking if they enjoyed their evening because he certainly did... Mike opened the door and immediately realized what had happened. The thief knew they went to dinner and used the opportunity to rob their home. This time, he stole Nancy's car, which was parked in the garage. The thief used a sophisticated social engineering technique. They created a two-stage attack, exploiting Mike and Nancy's natural greed (who would give up a free fancy dinner?) While Mike and Nancy are fictional characters, these events are based on a true story that happened in Ireland a few years ago. The "gentleman thief" struck several times. Most victims did not come forward because they were embarrassed by their gullibility. But truth be told, most of us can fall victim to social engineering.

Scams, Hacking, and Cybersecurity

Common Social Engineering Attacks:

Phishing, Examples and Warning Signs

The phonetic similarity between the word Phishing and the verb fishing is not a coincidence. A fisherman throws a net in the water to catch fish. Phishing is very similar. An attacker creates a fraudulent email message, which they use as bait, sends it to many people, and waits for someone to bite. At this point, the attack is not personalized or targeted toward an individual or a company. Phishing email tricks users into clicking on a link or downloading a file.

Phishing attacks have various purposes, including infecting the computer with data collection malware and spyware, disrupting regular operation, infecting the computer with ransomware for financial gain, collecting specific information that will later be used in a targeted attack for identity theft or impersonation. However, the latter is called a Spear Phishing attack (see below) because unlike a classic Phishing attack, it marks a specific target from the beginning.

We've all received a phishing email one time or another. Some are amateur-looking and are easy to detect even to an untrained individual, often because they are written poorly or use free translating tools, however, use of generative AI that has been booming since the end of 2022, allows social engineers to generate a compelling and professional looking content with ease. Some attacks are very sophisticated, and seemingly sent from a viable domain name, and use very similar to identical design as the service the attacker is spoofing.

Indications of a Phishing Email:

When you receive an email, you should look for common red flags that will help you identify a potential phishing email:

- Start by considering the email's general layout and formatting:
  - » Does it look professional? Does it use the correct logo, font, and design as the service it was allegedly sent from?
  - » Is the message relevant to you? If you've received an email from a credit card company, but don't have any of their cards, it is highly likely this is a phishing email sent to thousands of random email addresses, yours included.
- The email sender's address:
  - » An email address consists of two parts: the email prefix and the domain. For example: in the email address Mickey.Mouse@Gmail.com, *Mickey. Mouse* is the email prefix, and *gmail.com* is the domain. A legitimate email from a known service will ALWAYS use that service's domain. Established services will NEVER use public email addresses or other domain names such as – Gmail, Yahoo, Yandex etc. If the design seems legitimate but the sender looks suspicious – this is a tell-tale sign of a phishing email.
  - » Do you know the sender? Does this sender have a reason to contact you?
- Does the email address you by name? Legitimate services like PayPal, Amazon, and eBay, know your full name and will never start with a generic greeting such as 'Dear Customer,' 'Hello,' or 'Hello Customer.' An impersonal message is another sign of a

Scams, Hacking, and Cybersecurity

phishing email. Another potential phishing sign is a message that mentions your email address in an attempt to make it look more legitimate. The attacker already knows your email address, and it is very easy to create an automated script to add the recipient's email or prefix to the body of the message. This is not as definite indicator, but still, something to keep in mind and consider in the context of other potential signs of a phishing email.

- Spelling and grammar errors are another sign of a phishing email, especially when the message is supposedly from a known service. Legitimate and reputable companies use clear and correct language. Today, translation tools and AI text generating tools (e.g. ChatGPT, Preplexity, etc) make it easier than ever to craft emails using correct grammar, so correct English is not enough to determine the emails' authenticity.

- Writing Style: Is the writing style suitable for the sender? Does the writing style seem appropriate within context? Even if the sender is someone you know, it doesn't mean they actually sent this message. Many attackers use phishing techniques to hijack email addresses of legitimate users (tricking the users into typing in their email account credentials) and use these email addresses to further spread phishing emails to the victim's contacts, who might be less suspicious given the message seemingly came from a trusted sender. Does the message match the sender's writing style? Does the message make sense in the context of your relationship with the sender? Here again Gen AI makes it harder for us to detect those suspicious emails. With the right prompt it's easy to generate text that will look personal and authentic, however, we should be on the alert for non-consistencies with previous correspondence style.

- Email Signature: An email sent from a legitimate service (your bank, credit card company, e-commerce website, a service provider, etc.) will be signed by a specific person, provide the sender's contact details, and the design (logo, colors, etc.) will match the brand. An unsigned email or a signature that doesn't match the brand's style is another sign of a phishing email.

A phishing email could have all or only some of these warning signs. The lack of one of these signs doesn't make a message trustworthy, just as much as a single typo doesn't mean you've received a phishing email. To determine whether or not a message might be a phishing email, you should review each message individually and consider all the aspects described above.

Phishing Examples:

Nigerian Scam

The Nigerian Scam is one of the oldest types of scams. The scammers start by sending the victim an email promising a significant share of a large sum of money in return for a small up-front payment that will be used to obtain the large sum. The Nigerian Scam, which doesn't always originate from Nigeria, has many variants, some of the most common ones include a lawyer claiming the recipient is a long-lost relative of a wealthy businessman who just passed away and now the recipient stands to inherit a fortune, another example is a wealthy prisoner who asks for assistance in exchange of money, and many more.

The Nigerian Scam precedes the internet era, and back then, it was executed by posting letters. That's right, with stamps and mailboxes. Technology may have changed, but human nature hasn't. The same psychological traits that made us vulnerable then, are applicable now.

Scams, Hacking, and Cybersecurity

PRINCE JONES DIMKA
52/54 SHASHA ROAD, P.A.
DOPEMU - AGEGE
LAGOS - NIGERIA.
FAX: 234-1-521075

ATTENTION: THE MANAGING DIRECTOR

DEAR SIR,

URGENT BUSINESS PROPOSAL

WE HAVE THIRTY MILLION U.S. DOLLARS WHICH WE GOT FROM OVER INFLATED CONTRACT FROM CRUDE OIL CONTRACT AWARDED TO FOREIGN CONTRACTORS IN THE NIGERIAN NATIONAL PETROLEUM CORPORATION (NNPC). WE ARE SEEKING YOUR ASSISANCE AND PERMISSION TO REMIT THIS AMOUNT INTO YOUR ACCOUNT. YOUR COMMISSION IS THIRTY PERCENT OF THE MONEY.

PLEASE NOTIFY ME YOUR ACCEPTANCE TO DO THIS BUSINESS URGENTLY. THE MEN INVOLVED ARE MEN IN GOVERNMENT. MORE DETAILS WILL BE SENT TO YOU BY FAX AS SOON AS WE HEAR FROM YOU. FOR THE PURPOSE OF COMMUNICATION IN THIS MATTER, MAY WE HAVE YOUR TELEFAX, TELEX AND TELEPHONE NUMBERS INCLUDING YOUR PRIVATE HOME TELEPHONE NUMBER.

CONTACT ME URGENTLY THROUGH THE FAX NUMBER ABOVE.

PLEASE TREAT AS MOST CONFIDENTIAL, ALL REPLIES STRICTLY BY DHL COURIER, OR THROUGH ABOVE FAX NUMBER.

THANKS FOR YOUR CO-OPERATION.

YOURS FAITHFULLY,

PRINCE JONES DIMKA

3-4-95

Scams, Hacking, and Cybersecurity

As more people started to use the internet and access to information became simpler, scammers switched to email as the method of delivery. Nowadays, Nigerian scam messages can include personal details, the name of the recipient, and sometimes even other details that might give the impression the sender is a trusted entity, very similar to a spear phishing attack (see below).

By now everyone knows about the Nigerian scam. Why do scammers still use it? Well... the simple answer is that it still works.

The Nigerians scam is becoming increasingly sophisticated. Recently one of my friends received a message from someone claiming to be a lawyer handling the estate of an American businessman who was recently killed in a car accident together with all of his family, and that my friend is the only surviving relative that lawyer managed to track down. At first sight, that message looked more legitimate than your average phishing email: it was written in proper English with no errors, used the name of a real lawyer from the USA, and the fact it allegedly came from the USA tends to make people less suspicious, but it was a scam nonetheless.

Scams, Hacking, and Cybersecurity

9:17 AM (1 hours ago)

Waltham Estate Planning Law Firm
Address: Totten Pond Road Office Park 375
Totten Pond Road,
Suite 200 Waltham, MA, 02451/ USA/
Mobile: +1(267)668-6530
Email: kevin.ndolan11@hotmail.com

Dear ~~XXXX BEN-AMI,~~

I'm barrister Kevin Dolan, an attorney to late Mr. Michael BEN-AMI. A national of your country and a former director of (ConocoPhillips petroleum services) based here in United States (USA) and after shall be referred to as my Client.

Unfortunately, on 31st of January 2015, my Client, his Wife and his three children were involved in a car accident along West Stock bridge highway. All occupants of the vehicle unfortunately lost their lives.

He had an account valued ($18.7 Million U.S Dollars) and I have made several unsuccessful attempts to locate his relatives.

I am contacting you in trust because you have the same surname and nationality and to assist in repatriating the fund before it gets confiscated as an unclaimed fund.

Therefore I will stand here as your attorney to ensure the proceeds of this amount will be successfully transfer to your account and the I shall come over to your country for the sharing of the fund, 45% to me and 45% to you while 10% will be donated to the orphanage homes.

Your honest cooperation to enable us achieve this business is required from you. I guarantee that this will be execute under a legitimate arrangement that will protect you from any breach of law. U will need the following information from you to help us achieve this claim:

Your full name: _____
Address: _____
Your Age: _____
Occupation: _____
Your telephone, and mobile for Communication Purpose:
_____

Reply via my private email (kevin.ndolan11@hotmail.com) si that I can give you more details on the procedures.

Best regards
Kevin Neil Dolan Esq.

Another example that recently came to my knowledge had all the classic warning signs: a lawyer from Africa with the story of a $5 million inheritance. A vigilant relative of the 70-year-old target immediately realized it was a scam, the thing is that the scammer established a direct and personal line of communication with the target. The scammer communicated with the target via WhatsApp to create a false sense of trustworthiness. He even took it one step further and sent the victim an attorney certificate to prove he was a real licensed lawyer. Naturally, it was fake.

Even though the language the scammer used wasn't very professional, it took some serious effort, including a conversation with me, to convince the victim it was a scam and there was no fortune just waiting to be claimed.

Using WhatsApp and communicating with the victims to earn their trust, is not limited to phishing attacks. We'll discuss this in more detail in the 'Operation Rebound' chapter.

The use of various languages in various phishing attempts has become the new norm. Tools like Google Translate and ChatGPT, enable text generation in multiple languages, and looking for spelling mistakes and grammatical errors is just not enough when facing these tools.

Scams, Hacking, and Cybersecurity

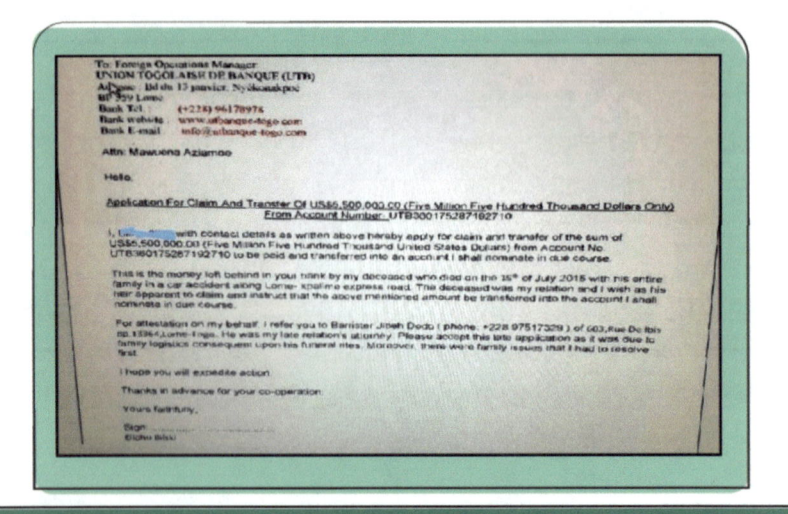

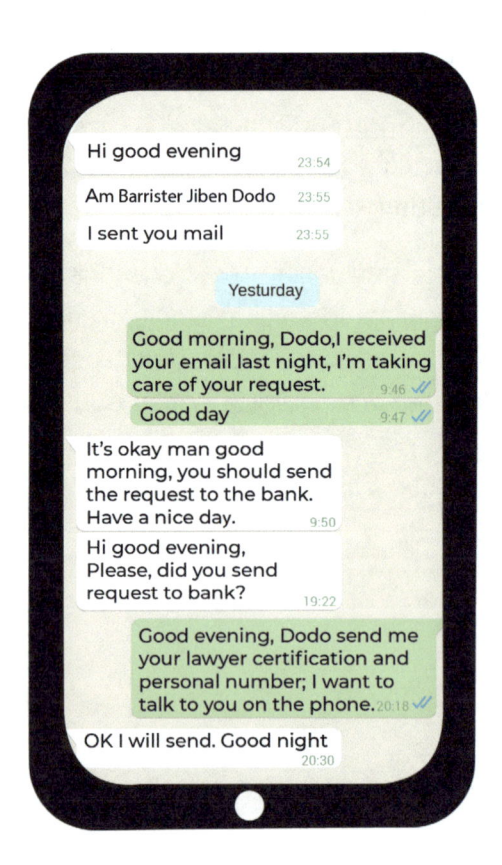

To: Foreign Operations Manager
UNION TOGOLAISE DE BANQUE (UTB)
Adresse : Bd du 13 janvier, Nyékonakpoè
BP 359 Lomé
Bank Tel. : (+228) 96178978
Bank website : www.utbanque-togo.com
Bank E-mail : info@utbanque-togo.com

Attn: Mawuena Aziamae

Hello,

**Application For Claim And Transfer Of US$5,500,000.00 (Five Million Five Hundred Thousand Dollars Only)
From Account Number : UTB300175287192710**

I, [redacted] with contact details as written above hereby apply for claim and transfer of the sum of US$5,500,000.00 (Five Million Five Hundred Thousand United States Dollars) from Account No. UTB300175287192710 to be paid and transferred into an account I shall nominate in due course.

This is the money left behind in your bank by my deceased who died on the 15th of July 2015 with his entire family in a car accident along Lome- xpalime express road. The deceased was my relation and I wish as his heir apparent to claim and instruct that the above mentioned amount be transferred into the account I shall nominate in due course.

For attestation on my behalf, I refer you to Barrister Jiben Dodo (phone. +228 97517329) of 603, Rue De Ibis np. 1334-I,Lomé-Togo. He was my late relation's attorney. Please accept this late application as it was due to family logistics consequent upon his funeral rites. Moreover, there were family reasons that I had to resolve first.

I hope you will expedite action.

Thanks in advance for your co-operation.

Yours faithfully,

Sign : _____
Elohin Bitsi

Hi good evening   23:54

Am Barrister Jiben Dodo   23:55

I sent you mail   23:55

Yesturday

Good morning, Dodo,I received your email last night, I'm taking care of your request.   9:46 ✓✓

Good day   9:47 ✓✓

It's okay man good morning, you should send the request to the bank. Have a nice day.   9:50

Hi good evening, Please, did you send request to bank?   19:22

Good evening, Dodo send me your lawyer certification and personal number; I want to talk to you on the phone.   20:18 ✓✓

OK I will send. Good night   20:30

Scams, Hacking, and Cybersecurity

Scams, Hacking, and Cybersecurity

How great is it that PayPal, Amazon, eBay, and many other services monitor our account activity as part of their fraud prevention effort.

Isn't it?

Big tech companies and financial institutes employ a variety of fraud prevention methods to protect their users from scammers. When attackers see an opportunity, they create similar messages to convince the users to click on the link and type their login credentials into a website spoofing the legitimate service.

These messages appear to have been sent by a legitimate and trusted service. The attackers shrewdly utilize the fear of fraudulent activity, money loss, or data theft and urgency ("If you don't take action within 24 hours, your account will be suspended"), which, as described in chapter 'The Threat of Social Engineering,' are effective motivators.

This type of attack is designed to steal the user's login credentials.

Why would an attacker want your credentials?

Well, you're not always the real target. Often, the real target is the company you work for, and your credentials will be used in a subsequent spear phishing attack (see below) targeting your co-workers.

This type of attack is no different from any other phishing email, and you should look for the same warning signs:

- The sender uses a public email address or a domain name that is different from that of the legitimate service.

- The message starts with a generic and impersonal greeting (such as 'Dear customer').

- Links to fake websites.

Scams, Hacking, and Cybersecurity

These fraudulent messages impersonate legitimate emails that companies send. As a result, poor language, spelling or grammar errors or a missing signature aren't as common. The attackers copy the content of the legitimate messages, rendering the scam harder to detect.

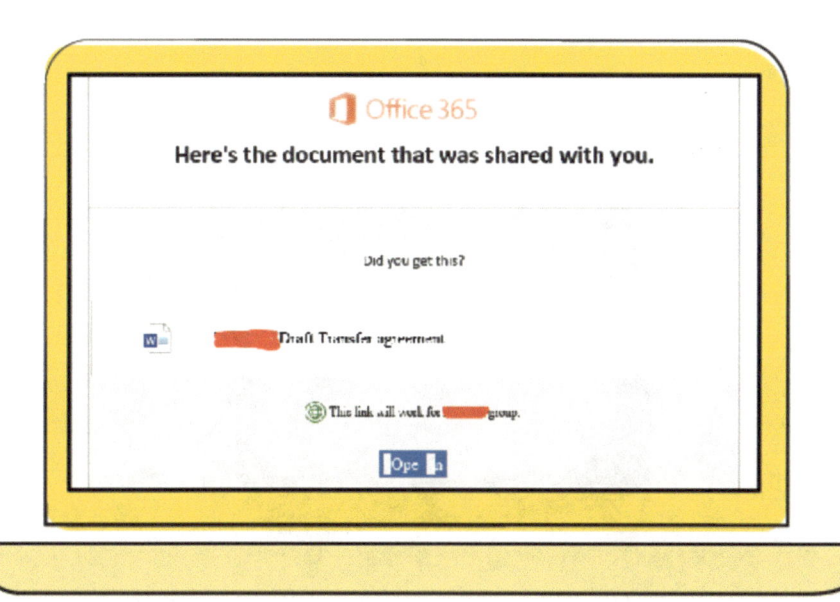

Office 365

Here's the document that was shared with you.

Did you get this?

Draft Transfer agreement

This link will work for ▓▓▓ group.

Open

In this case the sender's domain address is clearly not from Microsoft. Furthermore, the message is impersonal and calls to action (click a link). Examining the attached URL reveals that the link leads to a fake website designed to look like an Office365 login page, in an attempt to get the user to provide their credentials.

Scams, Hacking, and Cybersecurity

Another example is when the sender's address doesn't match the brand and immediately reveals this is a scam, not a legitimate message from PayPal. Upon a closer examination, we found other common warning signs: an impersonal generic greeting, abusing the receiver's uncertainty and fear, and urging the user to act immediately.

Track your Order

Similar to the login credential authentication phishing attack, attackers use common legitimate messages as the basis for their campaigns.

Order confirmation and order tracking are common types of phishing emails, particularly around the shopping season (Black

Scams, Hacking, and Cybersecurity

Friday, Cyber Monday, the holiday season) when the number of phishing attacks significantly increases.

Unlike login credential authentication phishing emails designed to steal users' login credentials as the first step in a bigger attack, order confirmation phishing emails are designed to trick users into clicking on a link and downloading malware to their devices. For example, downloading a ransomware to a workstation.

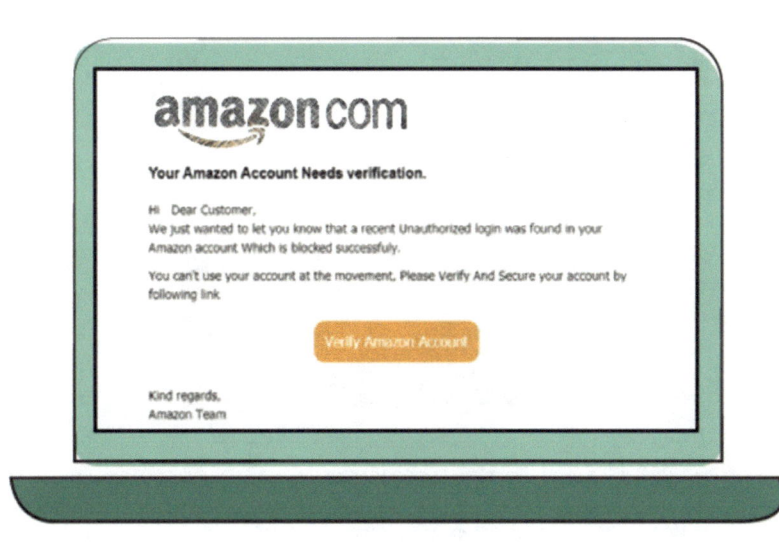

amazon.com

Your Amazon Account Needs verification.

Hi Dear Customer,

We just wanted to let you know that a recent Unauthorized login was found in your Amazon account Which is blocked successfuly.

You can't use your account at the movement, Please Verify And Secure your account by following link

[Verify Amazon Account]

Kind regards,
Amazon Team

Note how this order confirmation phishing email was sent after Black Friday. Reviewing the sender's details, however, quickly reveals this message was not sent by Amazon.

✳✳

Order confirmation phishing attacks aren't delivered only via email. Recently, the number of attacks targeting other communication methods has increased. For example: spreading malware through text messages (for more information, see Smishing). Here's a quick example of a smishing message:

Scams, Hacking, and Cybersecurity

> Text Message
> Friday 9:52 AM
>
> Hello mate, your FEDEX package with tracking code GB-6412-GH83 is waiting for you to set delivery preferences: c4dmc.info/sKenKPAAaLg

Do you find it believable that a company like FedEx would start a message with the informal greeting: 'Hello mate'?

One of the challenges with SMS phishing (smishing) is that tracking the sender is much more difficult. You can't hover the message with the mouse cursor to check the details as you do with email messages. Unfortunately, it's very easy to fake a text message sender credentials. Thus, if I send a text message and put "Amazon" as the sender, your phone will classify this message under other "Amazon" texts, so looking at the seder basically means nothing.

So, what should you do if you're actually waiting for a FedEx delivery?

Scams, Hacking, and Cybersecurity

> 💡 *Go directly to the vendor website, without clicking on any link in the message, and check if your shipment tracking number has any updates.*

Dr. David and Mr. Hyde

> ⚠️ 9:17 AM (1 hours ago)
>
> Good morning Dana,
>
> How are you? I hope this email finds you well. I need your help. I identified a company in the show that can supply the systems for the project. I need to immediately pay them a 70,000$ so that we will uphold the clients' timeline.
>
> Please transfer the funds to the attached account details ASAP.
>
> Thank you very much,
> David

Dana, the CFO, received the above message that was sent from the CEO's personal email address; he was attending a trade show in Germany at the time. She immediately became suspicious. She had been working with David for many years, and he was attending

Scams, Hacking, and Cybersecurity

a trade show looking for a specific solution for a client, but this wasn't how David spoke or wrote. David wouldn't say "How are you," "I need your help," or "Thank you very much!". David was a man of few words, who knows how to get things done. Dana always appreciated his direct communication style. Moreover, why was he telling her what the money was for? She knew why he was attending the trade show. Dana decided to call David and confirm his request before transferring the money.

David was having drinks with some colleagues when Dana called. At first, he didn't understand what Dana was talking about. The blood quickly drained from his face, as he realized an attacker hacked his personal email account, monitored his business correspondence, and finally impersonated him.

This reminded David of a similar incident in a rival company a couple of weeks earlier. It ended with the company transferring $120,000 to the scammer's account. He remembered how when he first heard the story, he thought *that could never happen to me*. His company invested a lot of money in its security systems, David completed a mandatory information security training program, how did the attacker manage to hack his email account?

This incident is proof that we're all vulnerable.

Thanks to her vigilance, Dana foiled the attack. She analyzed the message and noticed that David's writing style seemed different.

Attention to details, such as the use of nicknames, tone and voice, common expressions, and general writing style can help you identify phishing email.

Scams, Hacking, and Cybersecurity

The internet is like an elephant — it never forgets

In the sixth season of the TV show "The Good Wife", a photo of a congress candidate who was photographed in a compromising position with a statue had surfaced. The photo was taken when the candidate was in college and came back to haunt him years later.

The internet doesn't forget. What goes online - Stays online.

30 years ago, a teenager could do dumb things without worrying they'd follow them well into their adult life, today it isn't as simple. The world has changed. Teenagers today document everything they do: on Instagram, TikTok, WhatsApp, and a seemingly funny shenanigan at the age of 15, might prove to be very embarrassing years later. Especially, for instance, when applying for a senior management position or when running for office.

But we can't only blame teenagers for sharing too much online. We're just as guilty. A couple of months ago I came across a post written by a woman who was having an affair. She asked for advice on how to get away with it. She posted the question on a women's only group with tens of thousands of members. Could she have been certain that none of them knew her husband and that her secret would stay safe?

How often have you seen comments and posts originally posted in closed Facebook groups posted all over social media? Indeed, in many cases leaking information from a closed group violates the group rules. However, it's very naïve to believe that information posted to a group with thousands and sometimes tens of thousands of members could be considered private.

This risk isn't limited to online activity. How many stories have you

Scams, Hacking, and Cybersecurity

heard about people who went out for a vacation, only to find out they were robbed while they were away? This type of burglary takes place every day, and not because the burglars were flat out lucky. Burglars no longer lurk outside our houses, waiting for the lights to stay on all night. Instead, they lurk on social media, looking for people who post real-time photos from their current vacation.

GETTING READY FOR THE BIG DAY

GETTING BACK HOME

Social engineers look for information online and can create a targeted attack specific to the chosen victim, which brings us to the next type of phishing attack.

Spear Phishing

Similar to a diver who uses a speargun to hunt a specific fish instead of casting a fishing net in the hopes of catching some fish, a spear phishing attack targets a specific target.

The information we share online can be used against us. The more information we share, the easier it is for the attackers to create an attack tailored to us.

An attack targeting a specific company starts by _identifying_ key personnel in the company, based on data easily available on the company website's *About Us* page, or searching LinkedIn – the attacker begins researching those people. The attacker then creates an attack directed specifically at each key person.

If, for example, the attacker finds out that one of the executives is an avid marathonist, the attacker could use a marathon registration form or an ad for a special discount on running shoes as the basis for the attack. By clicking on the link in the message, the executive will be tricked into providing their login credentials or download malware that will give the attacker access to their email account.

Such attacks don't always target high level executives. In many cases, the attacker will choose a personal assistant who may have lower awareness, and yet, has access to a lot of sensitive information.

The first step of a targeted attack doesn't even have to be this sophisticated. A simple account detail confirmation message could be very effective with users who lack proper cyber security awareness.

In fact, it's a very common practice. A while ago, I received a call from an executive of a financial services company who fell victim to a spear phishing attack. The attacker managed to gain access to one of the top executives' email account. The attacker created an auto forward rule in the inbox, which forwarded a copy of all incoming emails to the email address the attacker was using, which allowed the attacker to follow everything that happened in the company[9]. When the attacker came across a message requesting to approve a large payment, the attacker impersonated the executive and sent a reply asking to transfer the money to a

Scams, Hacking, and Cybersecurity

different bank account "per the supplier's request," which was obviously a lie.

Luckily, in this case, the company's internal financial controls prevented the scam. However, dozens of other companies around the world lost significant sums of money after falling victim to spear phishing attacks.

Johnathan was sitting in a comfortable chair in the luxurious conference room on the 27th floor, when suddenly an email notification popped up on his smartwatch. Surprised, he looked up at Mike who was sitting in front of him. " Did you just go full millennial on me? Why would you text me when I'm right here?"

Mike didn't understand what Jonathan was on about, so Jonathan grabbed his smartphone, which was placed right next to him on the desk, and showed Mike the email in which he allegedly asked him to immediately transfer $1.5M to a subsidiary's bank account, whose details were attached.

Mike was the CEO of a US-based company, and Johnathan was the CFO of the company's UK offices. It just so happened that Johnathan was on a business trip in the States on the very same week Mike's email account was hacked.

This is yet another example of a spear phishing attack that was prevented by sheer luck. In 2016, the Belgian Bank Crelan wasn't as lucky, and a spear phishing attack resulted in a loss of over $75M. Facebook and Google reported losses of over $100M, and that's just the tip of the iceberg.

---

[9] Here's an easy fix – make sure your IT team disabled the option of auto-forward outside the organization.

Operation Rebound

In February 2020, the IDF published the details of what was dubbed operation rebound. It was a classic example of a social engineering attack. Hamas operatives posed as attractive young women on social media and tried to lure IDF soldiers. After texting for some time, the "women" suggested having a video call and sent a link for downloading the video call app. The app that the soldiers downloaded was malware that allowed the attackers to gain remote control over the device, monitor incoming and outgoing messages, and track the device's location.

This was not the first time Hamas used social media to lure IDF soldiers. The IDF had detected previous attacks and the soldiers who fell victim to the attacks were notified. This, however, marked another step up in the Hamas' ability to create fake online profiles and communicate with the soldiers in Hebrew, including sending voice messages in Hebrew to convince the soldiers they were talking with someone they could trust. This example is similar to the Nigerian scam (see: Phishing, Examples and Warning Signs), where the attacker communicated with the victim in English and even provided supporting documents to convince the victim the request was legitimate.

Here again I have to reference generative AI. If back in 2020 creating voice messages in Hebrew was a step up for Hamas, today generating voice or even video messages is simple, so vigilance is key!

Scams, Hacking, and Cybersecurity

Smishing, Examples and Warning Signs

Phishing attacks aren't always delivered by email. Recently, there's been an increased number of SMS phishing (Smishing) attempts. Smishing is a similar technique to phishing emails. It also invokes fear, urgency and greed, and is delivered via text messages.

Text Message — Today 01:15
Dear Customer,
Your AppleID is due to expire Today, Please tap http://bit.do/cRqb6 to update and prevent loss of services and data.
Apple smsSTOPto43420

SMS/MMS — Thursday, 2 November 2017
You received 3 Bitcoins (14 313,34 AUD) in your account, register immediately to accept the transfer.
https://goo.gl/Sy5pVo and
https://goo.gl/gTiQR3
10:32 am

17:52
[EE]:We were unable to process your latest bill. In order to avoid fees, update your billing information via: https://ee.uk.billing45.com/?ee=2

10:16 PM — +00 473234
Dear Customer,
Your bank's current account has been compromised, please click the following link to secure your account now
http://bn.mn/xtSf

16 Jun 2013 15:53
Important upgrade on your Mobile Account, kindly follow the link below.
www.███████.twfpr.com
Failure to comply might lead to suspension
███ Mobile

Attackers use Smishing to:

- Get the victim to provide personal information that the attacker can later use

Scams, Hacking, and Cybersecurity

- Infect the device with ransomware for financial gain.

- Infect the device with malware that gives the attacker access to private information, including the device's location, activity, contact list, and login credentials, for similar purposes as those of Operation Rebound.

As I previously mentioned, it's more challenging to determine whether a text message is legitimate or a scam. I strongly recommend refraining from clicking on any link received via a text message, and instead go directly to the website of the service that has allegedly sent you the message. Log into your account on the official website and check for any status notifications. Needless to say, if you've received text message from a bank or any other service you don't have an account with, you're clearly being scammed and should ignore the message.

> *Awareness and discretion are the best line of defense.*

Vishing

Guy was startled by a phone call. He was sitting at this desk, working on an urgent document for a client. He impatiently answered the call made by an unknown number.

"Hi Guy, this is Lisa from the fraud protection center of [his credit card company]. We've detected an unusual activity on your card, a 987 EUR payment made in Italy. Are you currently in Italy?"

Scams, Hacking, and Cybersecurity

Guy kept his cool. He wasn't in Italy nor has he bought anything online from Italy.

Lisa reassured Guy she will take care the false charge and asked him to confirm a few details including his full name, address, cell number, and ID number. Then, Lisa assured Guy that his card will be canceled, a new one will be sent to him, and that the 987 EUR charge will be refunded.

Before hanging up the call, Lisa asked Guy to reconfirm the last 8 digits of his credit card number. Feeling reassured by the call, and by the fact that Lisa has correctly given the first 8 digits of the card, Guy confirmed the card details, thanked Lisa, who wished him a good day and told him he should expect to receive the new card within 3 business days.

Three days passed, and since Guy hadn't received the new card, he called the credit card company. To his shock and horror, he discovered that during those three days, someone had used his card to make purchases worth tens of thousands of dollars.

The call Guy received from Lisa was Voice Phishing (or Vishing for short): a phishing attack conducted over the phone. Vishing is very common all over the world. The attacker researched the potential victim – Guy, gathered personal details about him and used them to give the call a sense of credibility. The attacker was probably sitting alone in a small room and playing call center sounds in the background, which can easily be found on YouTube.

Using personal details doesn't necessarily mean the attack was sophisticated. As you probably know, personal details such as, names, addressed, credit card numbers and bank account details of millions of people around the world have been leaked in multiple data breaches over the years.

Scams, Hacking, and Cybersecurity

If you want to see a live demonstration of a vishing attack, simply check out the following video[10] taken on the DefCon hackers convention in 2016.

The simplest and best way to avoid falling victim to a vishing attack is telling the representative you'll call them back. Then, hang up, go directly to the service provider's website, look for the official customer service phone number, and call the company.

Never trust the phone number that the alleged representative gave you or called from, because if this is indeed a vishing attack, you'll just end up calling the scammer.

Here again, I have to mention generative AI. Today it is simple to use a voice sample to regenerate audio that will sound authentic. This capability is widely exploited by criminals who use publicly available voice samples to impersonate people when communicating with their friends, families and colleagues. If you ever shared your voice online, for example on a story or reel, than it's out there available to be exploited.

---

[10] https://www.youtube.com/watch?v=lc7scxvKQOo

Scams, Hacking, and Cybersecurity

If you get a call from a family member or friend, asking you for money, a code or any other information you feel might be risky to share, it's advised to ask them some personal questions that only they will know.

Consequences:

So far, I presented several examples of attacks targeting both individuals and businesses. But what are the consequences of such attacks?

I've briefly mentioned some of the consequences but there are many more. To summarize:

CIA Triad Violations

As mentioned, the three basic information security principles are Confidentiality, Integrity, and Availability (CIA for short). If any of them has been compromised, it could result in dire consequences.

This chapter will review incidents in which Confidentiality, Integrity, or Availability have been compromised. These incidents are food for thought to raise awareness. Think about your circumstances and consider the threats most relevant to you and how to mitigate them.

Scams, Hacking, and Cybersecurity

Confidentiality Violation

We all have secrets; from an embarrassing teenage photo to a moment of infidelity, a medical condition we're ashamed of, a financial predicament, a sensitive personal detail, or some truly compromising information.

What if you're into BDSM and your boss learns about it. How would your co-workers respond?

Sometimes, the secret is something personal that could cause great inconvenience or embarrassment. No one wants their medical data to be publicly available, for example.

People can go to great lengths to protect the confidentiality of their data. Social engineers understand that and use sensitive information as leverage.

Twenty-year-old Johnathan had almost everything a young man of his age could wish for. He attended an Ivy League school, held a position at the school's newspaper, had a lot of friends, and even managed to save up enough money to buy a small car. There was one thing, however, that Jonathan had to address: his shyness. But he was determined to overcome this fault, and muster enough courage to ask a girl out.

Like other young adults, Johnathan spent a lot of time on social media. One day, as he browsed his favorite social media app, he met Sarah. She was a woman his age from a nearby city. They started texting, flirting. Johnathan was over the moon, and planned to ask Sarah out. After two days of texting and flirting, Sarah asked him to send a photo of himself. When he sent a photo of himself wearing a red T-shirt and a baseball cap, Sarah teased him a little and said she was expecting something more interesting...

Johnathan got the hint and sent her an intimate photo.

Scams, Hacking, and Cybersecurity

Then, everything changed. Sarah told him that she accessed his contact list and if he wouldn't pay her $400, she would send the picture to all of his friends, college dean, and even his boss at the newspaper.

Johnathan thought he was being pranked. But Sarah made it abundantly clear she was very serious. Confused, shaken, and completely betrayed, Johnathan paid Sarah then went to bed. How could this have happened? He thought this girl was into him.

When he woke up in the morning, he found another message from Sarah. She requested another payment, this time $500. Johnathan tried to protest, telling her he wasn't going to keep paying. Sarah replied with a screenshot of the email she would send his dean. In the email, she falsely accused Johnathan for sexually harassing her.

Panicking, because such an accusation could get him expelled, he promised to pay. He had only $220 in the bank. He called and parents, told them his car broke and asked them for money. His parents were surprised, Johnathan never asked them for money before, but he sounded so stressed they transferred $300 to his account.

Jonathan paid Sarah, who promised she wouldn't ask for more money. He was relieved.

Two days later, it seemed like Johnathan's life was back to normal. He attended his classes and then went out for a couple of beers with friends. When he returned home, he found a new message from Sarah: "I saw this amazing deal for these shoes I wanted, they're only $180...".

Johnathan realized Sarah will never leave him alone. He told her he had no more money and begged her to stop. "Tell it to someone who cares," Sarah laughed. "I want those shoes and you're going to buy them for me, or else..."

Desperate, distressed, scared, and drunk, he did the only thing that made sense to him at that moment, and hanged himself.

After Johnathan missed all his morning classes, one of his friends came looking for him around noon and found his body.

A couple of days later, the details of his suicide were uncovered. Investigators found the money transfers slips. They also found Johnathan's message to Sarah where he begged her to leave him alone, and a letter Johnathan left for his parents asking for their forgiveness if he had embarrassed them.

The attack Johnathan fell victim to is called Sextortion; a type of online blackmail where the victim is threatened that an intimate photo or video will be shared with other people. Over the years, many Sextortions have resulted in suicide.

This story is based on real events, altered to protect the privacy of the victim.

Scams, Hacking, and Cybersecurity

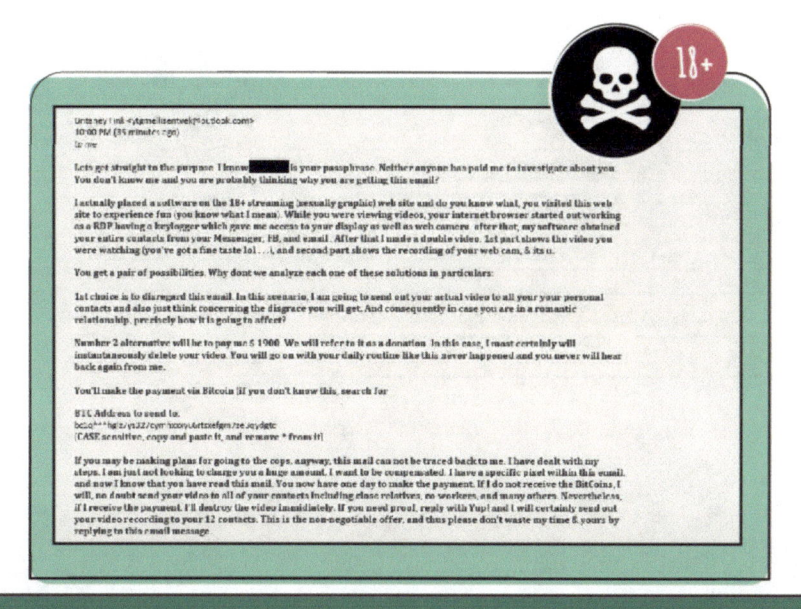

A Sextortion attack is not always targeted and continuous as in Johnathan's case. Sometimes a simple message does the trick:

Scams, Hacking, and Cybersecurity

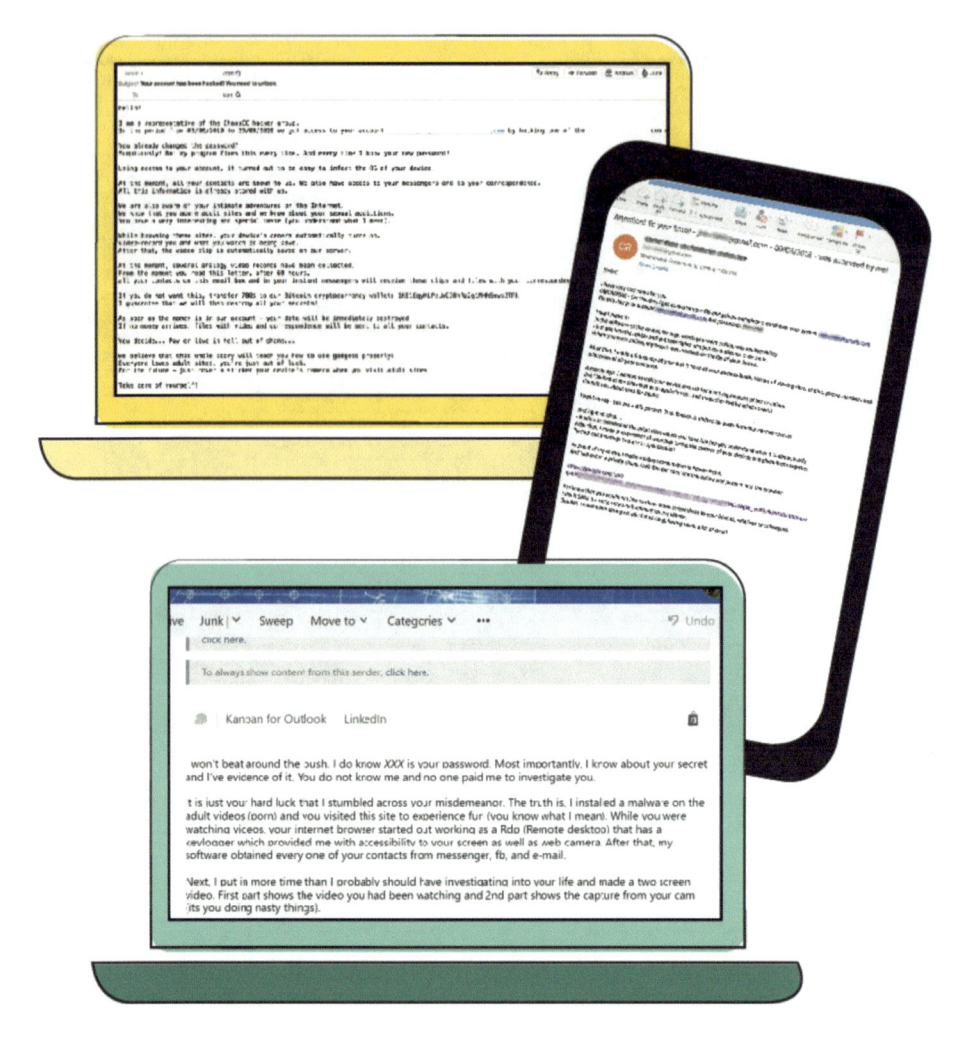

This message has different versions, but they all use shame as a motivator. The attackers use pseudo-technical terminology to explain how they managed to hack the victim's account.

Unlike the attack on Johnathan, these messages are non-personalized phishing emails that are sent to thousands of random people. The attackers don't care who the victims are as long as there are enough gullible people who will pay.

Scams, Hacking, and Cybersecurity

Usually, the messages include private details or information such as passwords to make the message more credible.

> HOW DO THEY KNOW MY PASSWORD IF THEY DIDN'T HACK ME?

To answer this question, let me introduce you to a very helpful website[11] called Have I Been Pawned (HIBP).

The site, founded in 2013 by Troy Hunt, an Australian cybersecurity expert, allows users to check whether their personal data has been compromised by data breaches.

---
[11] https://haveibeenpwned.com/

Scams, Hacking, and Cybersecurity

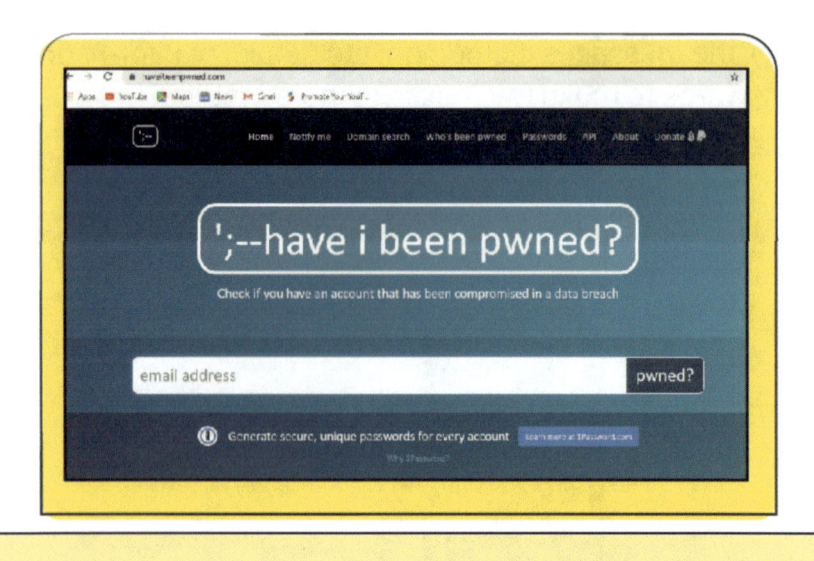

Searching for your email address will give you a list of all data breaches in which your email address was compromised.

Scams, Hacking, and Cybersecurity

Because data breaches are very common these days, I recommend adding your email address to the notification service thus you'll be notified if it was compromised by any new data breaches.

If your email address was compromised in a data breach, this means there is a database available somewhere on the web or the darknet with your email address and possibly, also your password. That's another reason why password reuse (using the same password in different accounts) is not a good idea. It's a single point of failure. We'll dive deeper into password management in the Passwords chapter.

Social engineers also like to use these databases because mentioning your password in their message makes it more credible. However, in some cases, social engineers rely on the limitations of our memory. Most people still use simple passwords. For example: passwords that contain your name, the names of your children, or pet, paired with your date of birth or similar details that are easy to guess.

If an attacker targeting a woman named Emma would search her on social media, he can reveal that her date of birth is May 14, 1989. If the attacker than includes a fictional password such as Emma140589!, Emma could easily misremember and be led to believe she has used this password in the past. She'll assume the attacker has her password and will be more likely to believe anything they say.

The purpose of this attack is usually financial, however, attackers can use similar elements to coerce the victim into performing certain actions.

Shame is a strong motivator, and one that hackers love using. Because we all have something we're ashamed of.

Scams, Hacking, and Cybersecurity

If you received a Sextortion message, whether it targets you specifically, like in Jonathan's case, or a generic message, this is how you should react:

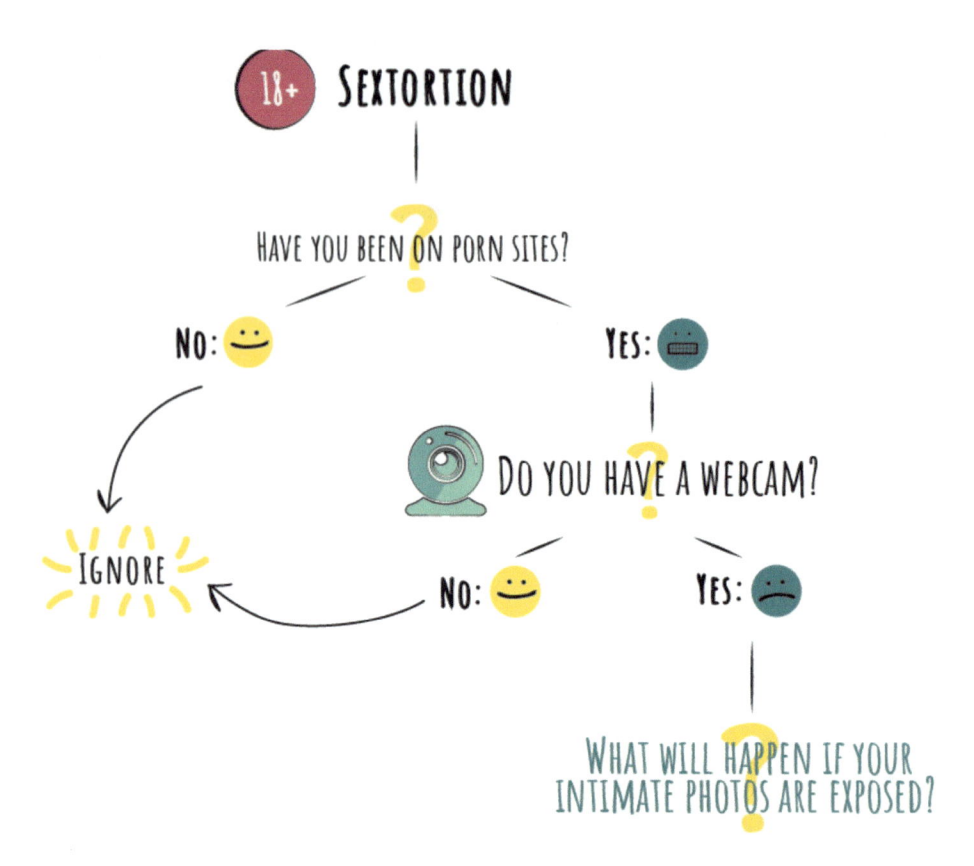

SEXTORTION

HAVE YOU BEEN ON PORN SITES?

- **NO:** → IGNORE
- **YES:** → DO YOU HAVE A WEBCAM?
  - **NO:** → IGNORE
  - **YES:** → WHAT WILL HAPPEN IF YOUR INTIMATE PHOTOS ARE EXPOSED?

Sextortion attacks have already resulted in dozens of suicides around the world and it's very important to raise awareness to this type of attack. What is the worst that could happen if the attacker releases my intimate photos, assuming they even have them?

Will I be embarrassed? Absolutely, but nothing most people can't move past.

Scams, Hacking, and Cybersecurity

Because the topic of this chapter is data confidentiality, I would be remiss if I ignored other types of sensitive or confidential information.

> **IT TAKES 20 YEARS TO BUILD A REPUTATION AND FIVE MINUTES TO RUIN IT. IF YOU THINK ABOUT THAT, YOU'LL DO THINGS DIFFERENTLY.**
> (WARREN BUFFETT)

"Fortunately, no one else knows about this," thought the CEO to himself as he was reading through the documents trying to figure out a solution to the critical fault recently discovered in the system the company is known for.

Suddenly, his office door flung open. The chief Technology officer came rushing in, trying to catch his breath. *"The press knows!"*

The report of the critical failure resulted in the company's stock plummeting to its lowest price in years.

But who leaked it? Everyone involved knew that if the word got out, it would be disastrous for the company.

Halfway around the world, the "investors" leaned back and delightfully watched as the stock price kept dropping. They took a gamble, and it paid off. They short sold the stock, and the drop in stock price made them millions of dollars[12]. In fact, **gamble** wasn't the right word in that case. They knew exactly when to sell the stocks because they were the ones who leaked the information

---

[12] Short selling is a method for making money on stocks whose price is decreasing.

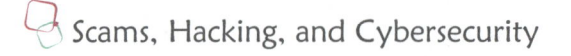

about the system's critical failure.

In December 2014, the Hacktivist group FIN4 launched a targeted attack to gather information about mergers and acquisitions that haven't been made public. The group used this information to turn a considerable profit in the stock market. They were not alone.

There are myriad ways hackers can get hold of confidential information:

- Blackmailing people who have access to this information. For example, using Sextortion to coerce the victim into divulging confidential information.

- Using phishing or spear phishing attacks to email accounts of strategic company personnel. By hacking into email accounts, the attackers gain access to all internal correspondence, which they use to gather inside information.

- Hacking companies working with a bigger company. Instead of hacking a specific company, hackers can target a law firm or an accounting firm working with companies of interest. Some firms specialize in mergers and acquisitions. Hacking the email address of an associate in such a firm could be very valuable as the attacker could learn about upcoming mergers and acquisitions long before they're made public. Furthermore, this enables the attackers to capitalize on mergers and acquisitions spanning many different industries, which makes it harder for financial regulators to detect this activity.

While the previous example was about business information, the following example is about a more relatable topic: personal information.

Scams, Hacking, and Cybersecurity

The first thing most people do when they go on vacation is post a selfie at the airport. They add a cute writing such as "on our way to a dream vacation in the Maldives." After all, what's the point of going on a dream vacation if not to share our experiences with our friends, especially if they're stuck at work while we're having the time of our lives? However, posting travel photos could also tip off people that our house is vacant. Creating the perfect opportunity to break in.

Scams, Hacking, and Cybersecurity

WHEN YOU'RE AWAY = THE BURGLAR IS ON HIS WAY!

Say CHEESE

But we don't have to travel to expose personal information. Checking in on social media when we go out to dinner could easily expose our location and our personal preferences.

Scams, Hacking, and Cybersecurity

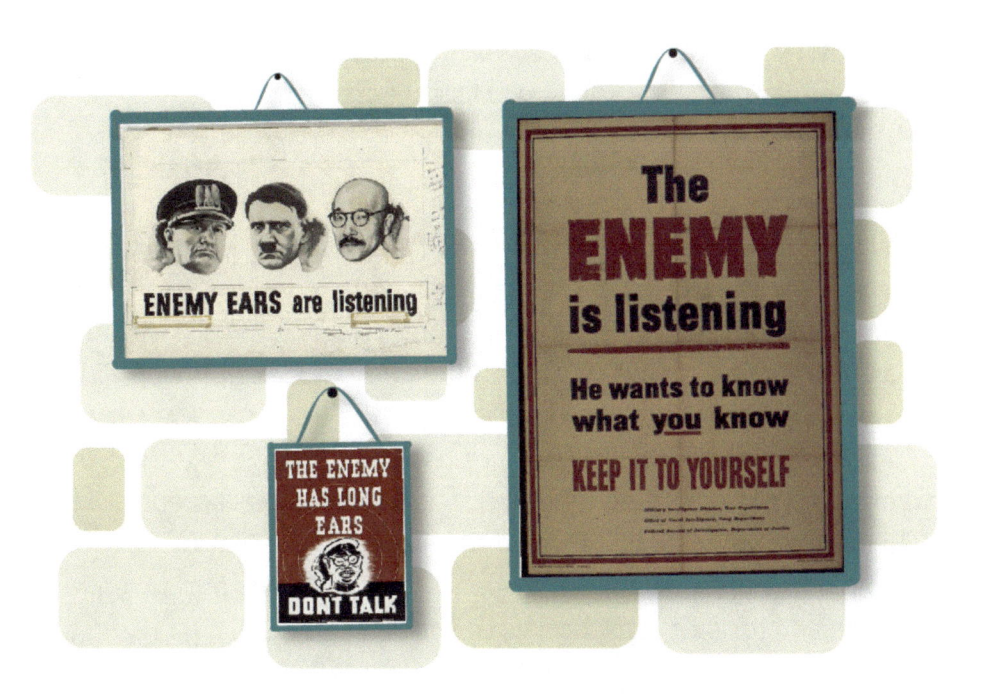

Similar campaigns warning people from divulging sensitive information that could be overheard are no new thing. The main difference is the medium. In the past, the biggest concern was eavesdropping, while today social media is a great source of confidential information. In many cases. Information shared unwittingly on social media, can be exploited by wrong doers. Operation Rebound is a good example of that.

Military operations were canceled multiple times because soldiers revealed confidential information about the operation. Back in the late 90s, when cell phones became more widespread, there were cases of IDF soldiers in the south of Lebanon who sent text messages to family and friends informing them when they'll be back home, thus exposing schedules and progress.

Scams, Hacking, and Cybersecurity

As many applications automatically tag the location of the user, this can be a recipe for disaster.

Almost everyone is occasionally guilty of posting personal information, thus, almost everyone will have to face the consequences.

--- ✶✶ ---

What does Jennifer Lawrence, Kate Upton, Ariane Grande, Kirsten Dunst, Avril Lavine, and Hilary Duff all have in common? Yes, they're all celebrities but that's not what I mean. Intimate photos of them, as well as others were leaked to the internet in September 2014. The photos were obtained by breaching the cloud storage service Apple iCloud, and to this day are used as a cautionary tale. The photos were stored on the celebrities' private cloud accounts, yet a security vulnerability allowed the attackers to steal the images, post some samples on the imageboard 4CHAN, and put the entire collection for sale in exchange for Bitcoin.

On the same week that the data breach made headlines, Cosmopolitan magazine conducted a survey among 850 female readers whose average age was 21. According to the survey, 99% of the female participants have taken intimate photos of themselves at some point, however, 25% answered that they've taken intimate photos, but they could not be recognized in them.

86% of the participants said they don't regret taking intimate photos. Though 91% of them never had those intimate photos leaked to a broader audience.

HAVE YOU EVER TAKEN AN INTIMATE SELFIE?

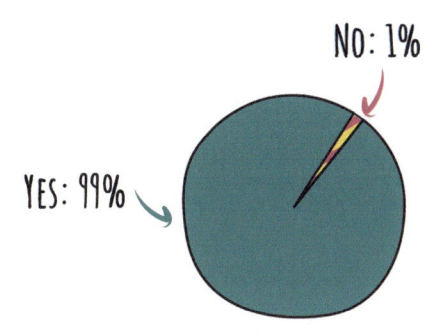

NO: 1%

YES: 99%

The Cosmo Survey proved that telling people "Don't take intimate photos of yourself" is simply irrelevant. We live in the age of social media, and photos, including intimate photos, are part of the deal.

A guy meets a girl, they fall in love, exchange intimate photos and sometimes even sexually explicit videos.

But what happens when they break up?

Meet a new pornographic genre:

Revenge Porn

In the 80s, the pornographic magazine Hustler introduced a new section featuring explicit intimate photos taken by amateurs and submitted by readers. Most readers submitted photos of themselves or their partners. The photos often included details about the person in the picture: name, city, occupation, and sometimes even hobbies. However, some readers submitted the photos as a way of taking revenge on their ex. The magazine didn't always verify that the person in the picture gave their consent and was consequently sued several times.

Scams, Hacking, and Cybersecurity

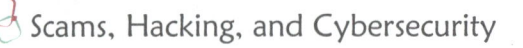

> **!** *Did your girlfriend cheat on you? Your boyfriend dumped you? It's time for revenge!*

Like most things these days, the revenge porn genre went online. A growing number of websites dedicated to revenge porn popped up on the web. One that garnered media attention was YouGotPosted, which allowed users to upload revenge porn photos. The website owners realized they could make a lot of money, and launched another website called ChangeMyReputation, where victims of YouGotPosted could pay to remove their photos from the YouGotPosted site.

Now that's audacious!

Both YouGotPosted and ChangeMyReputation were taken down in 2013. Since then, new revenge porn sites took their place and new laws banning revenge porn continue to emerge.

While revenge porn may not strictly qualify as an information security issue, it illustrates how information we post or share with others can be used against. It was also important for me, as a mother of three, to raise awareness to the subject.

If we all **count to 10** before taking a potentially compromising or explicit photo or a video and sharing them with someone else, perhaps we can reduce revenge porn incidents. If parents discuss this issue with their teenagers, maybe fewer teens will readily exchange explicit photos that could fall in the wrong hands.

It should be noted that we have to remember to see the bigger picture. Sure, compromising pictures could cause a great deal of public embarrassment, but what's the worst that could happen?

For the majority of people that's where it ends. Unless we ourselves treat it as more.

Identity Theft

On the one hand, identity theft is a huge issue; I could easily dedicate a whole chapter, perhaps even an entire book to this subject. However, identity theft is not a "classic" information security issue. On the other hand, almost all identity theft incidents start with breaching confidentiality. Information that we thought is personal and private leaks and is used against us by various entities or people with whom we are in contact.

"Hello, thank you for calling [company name]. Steven speaking, how may I help you?"

When you call customer service or technical support, you're asked to verify your identity. Usually, the agent asks for your full name, ID number, address, and a few other questions to verify who you are. Many companies send a one-time code via a text message to the telephone number you've provided when you created your account.

By now you know that information such as your name, ID number, and address are details that any attacker can obtain quite easily, and therefore these questions aren't a reliable identity verification method.

Identity theft may be used to commit fraud or crimes under your name or to establish trust and credibility as part of a continuous spear phishing attack against another target, such as your workplace or someone you know.

Because most of us aren't interesting enough to justify the time and effort required to steal our **personal** identity, we tend to ignore the risk. As you probably know by now, attackers often

Scams, Hacking, and Cybersecurity

select targets not because they have a special interest in them, but because these targets can serve a purpose and facilitate a larger targeted attack.

Given how common data breaches have become, you should assume that at least some of your personal information has been leaked and that you're at risk for identity theft.

How can we protect ourselves against identity theft:

Regularly review bank and credit card statements

Think twice before adding personal details to online forms and services

Review friend requests on social media and approve them only if you know the requester

Stay vigilant!
If you receive an unexpected email, text message or friend request – review them and look for warning signs.

Data Integrity Failure

Failure of data integrity could have serious ramifications, from financial, such as is in the story I shared at the beginning of this book, when my bank account was foreclosed, to risking human lives, for example due to out-of-date medical records.

One of the most common concepts in computer science is *Garbage In, Garbage Out,* meaning that flawed input data will result in flawed output data.

Not every data integrity failure is the result of tampering. Sometimes it's the result of user laziness. For example, when entering the details of a new customer into the system:

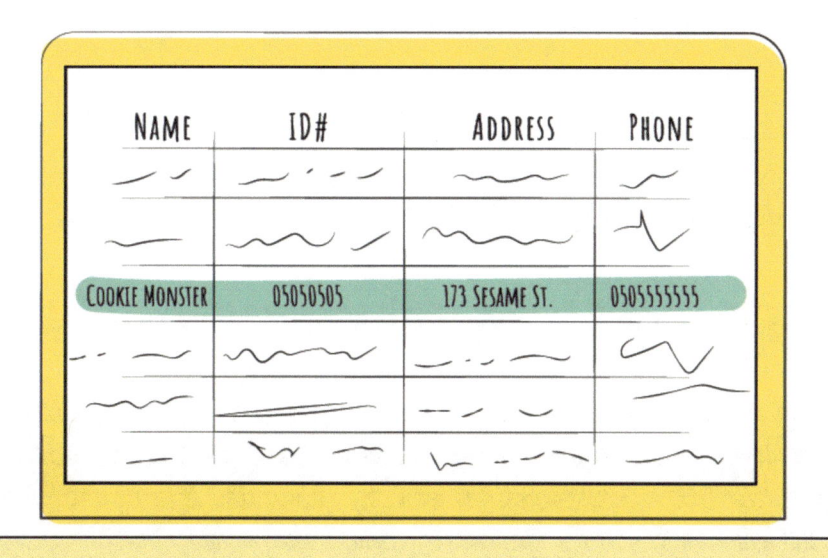

If I've entered incoherent data, it's no wonder that when I'll try to retrieve data, I'll end up with a useless output. It should be noted that most computer systems implement controls to avoid data entry errors, mistakes, and incomplete data. For example, verifying an address against an address database, verifying the check digit of an ID number, and so on. These controls are designed to detect and prevent human data entry errors. But what happens when the data is tampered with?

Wouldn't it be great if you could park anywhere you wanted, and then hack the system and cancel all the parking tickets you've received? And what if you decide to turn a profit and start a small business offering family and friends this wonderful and highly illegal service for a small fee? After all, hackers need to make a living too. However, the local municipality in question, will probably be less enthusiastic about this endeavor.

If I can't trust the accuracy of the data in my system, there's no point using it to begin with.

Sometimes the integrity of the data can affect tens of thousands of people, especially when financial data is involved. The next story is an excellent example.

"I have a once-in-a-lifetime investment opportunity for you! Invest in an energy company that keeps growing every quarter, with around 20,000 employees, ranked number one in the "Top 100 Companies to Work for" list, and over the last two years, its share price soared from $20 to $90. All my clients invest in this company, except one who's still kicking himself for ignoring my advice last year."

Sounds like a great investment, right? In the late 1990s, similar conversations took place in investment firms all over the US. The specific company in question was Enron. Back then, Enron was THE stock to invest in. Everyone wanted to own Enron shares. Kenneth Lay, the founder, and Jeffrey Skilling, the CEO, were said to have the Midas touch.

Scams, Hacking, and Cybersecurity

ENRON'S REVENUE (IN MILLIONS)

REVENUE (MILLION $)

STOCK PRICE

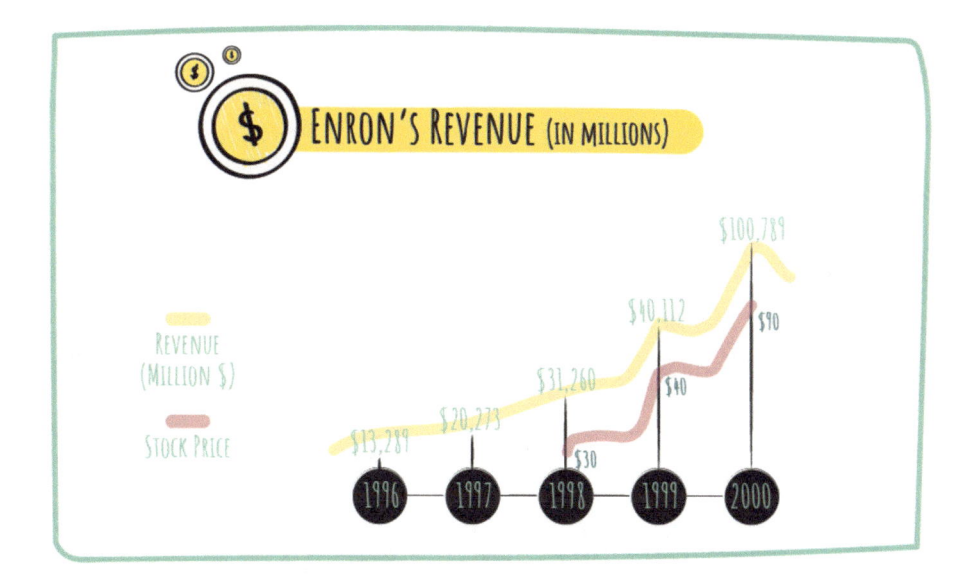

	1996	1997	1998	1999	2000
Revenue	$13,289	$20,273	$31,260	$40,112	$100,789
Stock Price			$30	$40	$90

However, the figures Enron reported were based on an accounting method called Mark-to-Market, meaning the company reported the projected income even if the money was yet to be received. For example: in 2000 Enron signed a 20-year contract with Blockbuster, with estimated profits of $100M that were immediately put on the books. Enron had also transferred debts to non-traded subsidiaries to hide them from the shareholders. These were just a few of the accounting tricks the company used, which had allowed it to continue to claim impressive growth figures even though their actual performance was quite the contrary.

In other words: Enron cooked the books.

Where were the accountants and auditors, the ones whose job it was to identify accounting frauds?

Enron has been working for years with the leading accounting firm Arthur Andersen, who failed to report the fraud after Enron executives bribed the auditors and convinced them to conceal the actual figures from the public.

Scams, Hacking, and Cybersecurity

In late 2000, the CEO, Skilling left the company. A few months later, the Federal Trade Commission launched an investigation into Enron, revealing the complex accounting fraud.

As the days went by, the depth and details of the fraud became clearer, and by the end of 2001, Enron's stock price plummeted from almost $90 per share to mere cents. The company filed for bankruptcy in December 2001. To this day, Enron's bankruptcy is ranked as one the top 10 biggest in the history of the United States.

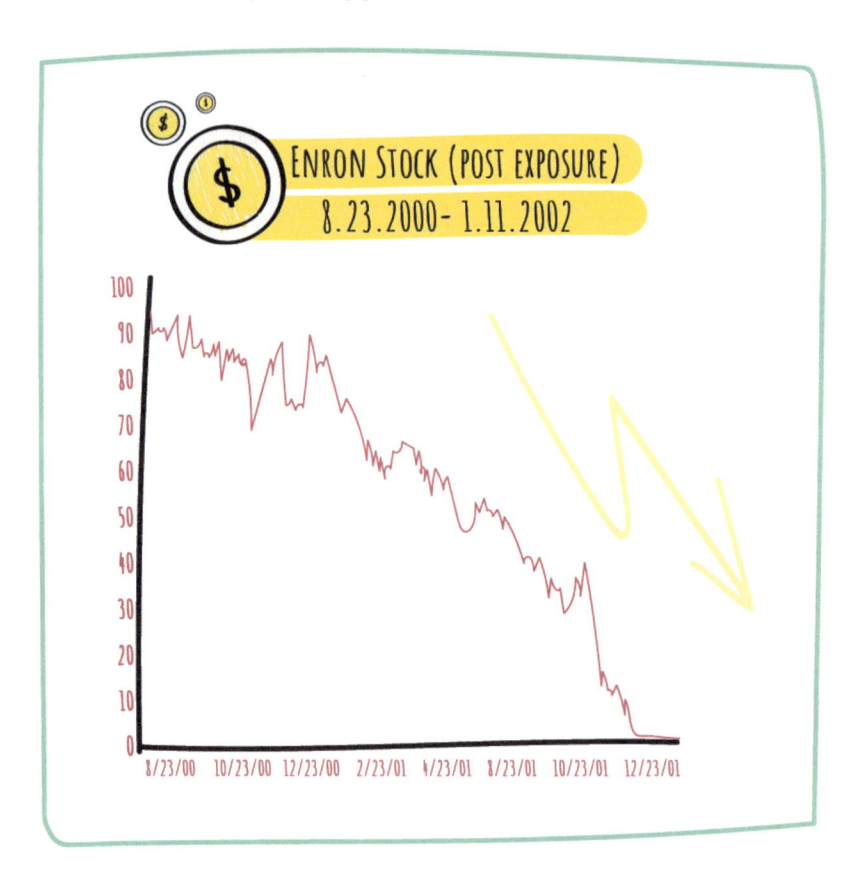

ENRON STOCK (POST EXPOSURE)
8.23.2000 - 1.11.2002

Scams, Hacking, and Cybersecurity

In the days that followed...

Kenneth Lay (founder, chairman and CEO) was convicted on ten counts of securities fraud. He died of a heart attack three months before his scheduled sentencing.

Jeffrey Skilling (former president, COO, and CEO), was convicted of federal felony charges, and sentenced to 24 years in prison. He was released in 2019 after having served 12 years.

Tens of thousands, from companys' employees to the general public, had lost their investments, including their pensions.

Arthur Andersen, who was one of the BIG5 accounting firms at the time, did not survive the scandal and collapsed in 2002

The US senate had passed the bipartisan federal Sarbanes-Oxley Act (SOX) that aims to assure scandals such as Enron will not reoccur. The act mandates certain practices in financial record keeping and reporting for publicly traded organizations.

Scams, Hacking, and Cybersecurity

The Enron scandal is a classic example of accounting fraud, but it's also a great example of the risks associated with data integrity failure — one of the three information security principles of the CIA triad. Indeed, during the Enron scandal, the information systems didn't perform data integrity checks as they do today, thus enabling the company to manipulate the accounting data, which ultimately led to its downfall.

The Trade Bank Embezzlement

The Trade Bank embezzlement is one of the biggest financial scams in the history of Israel.

From 1997 to 2002, Etti Alon, who was the Deputy Chief of Investments at the time, embezzled a total of $65M from the now defunct Trade Bank.

Alon embezzled the money to help her brother, Ofer Maximov, pay off his gambling debts.

She successfully pulled off the fraud by employing two methods:

3. Issuing fake loans to bank customers, typically a balloon loan using the customers' real savings as a guarantee.
4. Breaking customers' term deposits and transferring the money around several accounts to hide the transfer.

Alon changed the contact details of the bank customers to hide her scam, and issued fake letters to the customers whose accounts she embezzled.

The fraud was enabled by structural administrative and technological failures, which prevented the bank management and employees in key roles from detecting the fraudulent activity.

For example:

- *There was no separation of duties, allowing Alon to open accounts and both apply for and approve a loan all by herself without requiring the approval of another key bank personnel.*

- *No rotation of employees in sensitive positions: following the scandal, the Bank of Israel directed all banks to rotate employees between assignments, positions, and even locations to improve internal fraud prevention controls.*

- *Mandatory vacations: Etti Alon refused to take time off, not even a sick day, during the entire embezzlement period. She feared that if she were to be replaced someone might notice something was amiss. As a result of the scandal, current Bank of Israel regulations force bank employees in certain positions to take a couple weeks of continuous time off to increase the likelihood of uncovering any irregularities in time.*

The Trade Bank scandal and the global ramifications of the Enron scandal, led to the legislations of various acts and directives to reduce the risk of fraud and enhance security practices.

Following the embezzlement, The Israeli Banks Commissioner published Directive 357 — Information Technology Management, addressing the aforementioned issues, as well as information security risk assessment, information security roles and responsibilities, encryptions, backups, passwords, and more.

Failure of Data Availability

Throughout the years, many information security experts objected to the idea that backup is an intrinsic part of information security. I believe that if the information is not available when needed, it doesn't matter how well you've secured it because you can't use it. At the beginning of the book, I mentioned that Availability is the third fundamental principle of the information security CIA triad (alongside Confidentiality and Integrity).

Backups are an easy way to ensure information is available when needed. Backing up your data doesn't have to be complicated, and contrary to common belief, is not something only system administrators should worry about. Backup could be as simple as copying your presentation file to a flash drive or emailing a copy of the presentation to the event organizers.

There are multiple threats to data availability, including:

- Theft or loss of mobile devices
- Technical fault
- Loss of access to the data
- Malware infection, including ransomware

In this chapter, I'll explore a few stories about data availability failures, caused by both physical and logical damage, and suggest a couple of methods I use to minimize the risk.

Physical Damage

Mobile devices are often physically damaged.

I always say I don't deserve a nice smartphone because I keep breaking them.

Physical damage could be temporary and repairable, a cracked phone screen, for example. Granted, you'll have to live somehow without your phone for a couple of days while it's being repaired. But you'll get it back as good as new. However, physical damage can also be unrepairable, such as a serious fall that completely

Scams, Hacking, and Cybersecurity

destroys the device or water damage. The same goes if you simply lose the device.

Remember Murphy's Law: If something can go wrong, it will.

It was Monday morning. I was still a little jetlagged from the weekend. There were 17 new messages waiting in my inbox.

Coffee, I needed coffee.

I headed for the office kitchenette, made myself a nice cup of coffee, and sat at my desk. As I browsed my inbox, I reached for my coffee mug, and…

SPLASH! I accidentally hit the mug and tipped it over, spilling the coffee all over my desk, keyboard, documents and phone.

We've all been there. We've spilled a cup of coffee all over our desk, dropped our laptop bag, or forgot to close a water bottle that started dripping all over our belongings, phone, and wallet.

And of course, that one time, our phone fell into the 🚽.

These are all common causes of physical damage. If you fail to plan ahead and back up your data, this type of physical damage could easily lead to data loss. Not to mention the frustration and aggravation resulting from losing important data.

The office space of the investment firm spanned multiple stories in one of the Twin Towers at the World Trade Center. As the firm grew, it required more office space. The Chief Information Officer advised they move some of their operations to the other tower, and so they did. Why was the CIO involved in selecting the location of the office? It's simple. The CIO wanted to establish an offsite location for backups — a separate physical location from the main information system to which all the business data is replicated — and using the other tower would significantly reduce the setup cost compared to a new location in a completely different location. Replicating the data between the offices in the twin towers created redundancy that would allow the company to continue working in case of a server failure or physical damage to the server room in one location.

Furthermore, per the risk assessment, there was basically zero chance of a massive failure or damage hitting both towers at the same time. According to the engineering assessments, the Twin Towers were both earthquake-proof and a fire couldn't spread from one tower to the other.

The company approved the plan, leased new office space, built a new and advanced server room to spec, and connected the two server rooms with a dedicated networking infrastructure to replicate the data continuously.

Then the 9/11 attacks happened. The Twin Towers could withstand an earthquake. They could survive a fire; but not two planes crashing into them.

In addition to the tragic loss of lives, the company also lost all its data as both server rooms were destroyed in the attack.

As mentioned, the chance of both towers collapsing at the same time seemed implausible, Silverstein Properties Inc. — the company that owned the Word Trade Center at the time — took out insurance policies covering only one occurrence.

Silverstein Properties Inc. then claimed double the insurance money, arguing that each airplane strike was a single occurrence, whereas the insurance companies argued both planes were considered as one occurrence. The insurance dispute went to court, and after years of deliberations, the court ruled in favor of the insurance companies.

These days, companies are advised to set up the offsite backup location 30 to 100 miles (50 to 160 Km) away from the main site.

Recently I came across[13] an interesting anecdote about operating the AMOS communication satellite. In 1996, early into the AMOS project, the Israel Aerospace Industries (IAI) built a command center designed to operate 24/7 with all the communication and control systems and an antenna site.

A group of experts was charged with devising a backup strategy to maintain data integrity and availability and ensure continuity of operations.

After many debates, the team decided to proceed as follows: There shall be two backup sites:

1. *Hot site where all data from the main site would be replicated in real time, and operational readiness would be checked and verified every day. The backup hot site was built 3 miles (5 Km) away from the main site, to reduce the risk that a force majeure event would hit both sites simultaneously.*

2. *Remote backup site, a secondary cold site built more than 60 miles (100 Km) away to ensure the continuity of operation in case the first two sites were damaged. The cold site got periodic data backups from the main site and was created as an additional protection layer.*

---

[13] Many thanks to Meidad Pariente for sharing this story with me.

Scams, Hacking, and Cybersecurity

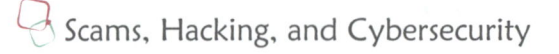

The guidelines were strictly followed and proved themselves on several occasions.

---- ✹✹ ----

The news about the death of the head of the division left the employees shocked. He was one of those people who everyone knew, the type of manager who knew all the division members' names, who participated in water cooler talks, and expressed genuine interest in the professional and personal lives of the many people working under him.

The funeral was scheduled for Thursday at 4 PM, and around half past 3, a long convoy of company staff set off towards the cemetery.

While the late manager's son gave the eulogy and the attendants followed the coffin in silence to its final resting place, a group of car burglars swiftly broke into the company car trunks, and stole their contents.

When the employees returned to the cemetery parking lot, they discovered that dozens of laptops had been stolen while they were attending the funeral.

Thieves these days plan ahead. They no longer lurk in the shadows, waiting for random opportunities; these days, they do recon. The obituary that the company published the morning of the funeral was just the type of information the thieves look for: a big high-tech company, the death of a senior executive, and a funeral on a *Thursday* afternoon. They knew most employees wouldn't return to the office after the funeral, meaning people would likely bring their work laptops and leave them in the car until the funeral was over.

Cemeteries and event venues parking lots are popular targets for car burglars. They look for cars with a company logo, trusting that

Scams, Hacking, and Cybersecurity

people leave their laptops in the car while they're at the event.

A stolen device could cause two types of security breaches:

- Confidentiality
- Availability

Since most cases of laptop or mobile device theft aren't associated with business espionage, the risk of data breach can, and should be mitigated.

If you haven't locked your laptop, smartphone, or tablet with a PIN/password, thieves might be tempted to look at the information. If you have confidential or sensitive information on the device, thieves might use it for blackmail, sell it to competitors, or personal use.

In recent years there were two incidents where someone managed to jam the communication channels with two US satellites for several minutes at a time. After the information leaked to the media, an investigation was launched and found that foreign agents managed to steal a couple of NASA laptops in the months leading to the incidents.

NASA employees take pride in their workplace and usually walk around airports wearing bags, caps, and shirts with the NASA logo. Consequently, they're easy targets for foreign operatives waiting for an opportunity to steal their laptops.

The confidentiality threat could be solved using two simple methods:

Data encryption Various free or inexpensive encryption solutions are available today, protecting information from unauthorized access in case the device is stolen.

Scams, Hacking, and Cybersecurity

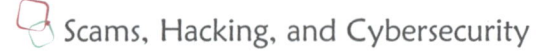

Set up a strong password or two-factor authentication. It's strongly advised to secure mobile devices with a password or biometric authentication to minimize the risk of unauthorized access to personal or sensitive data in case the device is lost or stolen.

Advanced tool:

Automatically erase data: some mobile devices offer an automatic data erasing option after a set number of consecutive failed password entry attempts. The default is usually nine consecutive attempts, after which all the data stored locally on the device is erased.

Maintaining data availability is much simpler and straightforward: *an up-to-date backup of your data* protects you against data loss if your device is lost or stolen.

Logical Data Loss

Most of us tend to ignore the risk of fire, flooding, earthquake, and other types of disasters, although statistically, these disasters are more frequent than we believe, and data backup reduces the impact of such events. Conversely, we all recognize the risk of a logical data loss, which occurs when the data becomes inaccessible due to deletion or malware such as ransomware.

I've covered the basics of ransomware in the common threats chapter. Next, I'll share stories about the impact of ransomware attacks, and their global impact, where they're most likely to occur in our personal and professional life.

A Ransomware Incident — the Personal Angle

The Photographer

A few of years ago, I was tagged on a Facebook post uploaded by a video photographer who lives near me. She posted a screenshot of a suspicious message she got on her computer. It was a ransomware notice. All her files got encrypted, including dozens of raw and edited footage files.

The attackers asked for $200 to unlock the encrypted files.

I asked if she had a backup of all her important data. She didn't. She told me that a computer technician in a nearby city offered to try and restore the data for a couple of hundred dollars. Because the type of ransomware that infected her computer was new, there was no public decryption key available, which meant paying the computer technician was akin to throwing money to the wind because he wouldn't be able to decrypt her data. The data was critical for her business; it was raw footage that couldn't be recreated. I recommended her to pay the ransom. I'm a strong advocate for not paying ransom but considering that the data was critical to her work, there was no public decryption key in sight, the attack was from a known group, and the data wasn't backed up — the pragmatic way to salvage the data was to pay the ransom.

She didn't take my advice. She paid the computer technician, who despite doing his best, failed to restore the data. Eventually, she was forced to pay the ransom. Luckily for her, these attackers were true to their word and sent her the decryption key after they received the ransom payment.

Scams, Hacking, and Cybersecurity

After she decrypted her disk and restored the data, I gave her a few tips and recommendations for keeping her data safe and sound, minimizing the risk, and identifying warning signs. I encouraged her to back up her data so she wouldn't find herself at the mercy of attackers even if her computer would be infected with ransomware again. You can find these tips and recommendations in the Backups chapter.

Ransomware Incident

NotPetya and MAERSK — the Organizational Angle

At the end of June 2017, reports surfaced worldwide about a new and quickly spreading ransomware attack targeting organizations. The way the ransomware spread was very similar to the WannaCry[14] ransomware used earlier that year, which was no coincidence. The Petya ransomware was using the same vulnerability exploit believed to have been developed by the NSA and was used months earlier in the WannaCry attacks.

Early on, researchers thought it was a new variant of the PETYA ransomware, but it turned out to be a similar yet different type of malware. Therefore, it was aptly named NotPetya.

The ransomware attack hit some of the world's largest corporations, including Maersk, Merck, FedEx, and Mondelez International.

In the afternoon of June 27, 2017, the helpdesk at Maersk headquarters, the world's largest container ship and supply vessel operator, was flooded with requests for help. An increasing number of people gathered around the helpdesk with their laptops. All their screens had an ominous message written in red letters against a black background.

---

[14] WannaCry will be covered shortly

Scams, Hacking, and Cybersecurity

Your important files are now encrypted... if you want them back pay us $300.

Everybody left work that day confused and under a cloud of uncertainty. When will they be able to get back to work? What happened to their computers?

Meanwhile, the workday has begun in a New Jersey seaport. Dozens of trucks lined up at the entrance to the terminal, but the computers running the port's information systems were also down. After hours of waiting and a line of trucks that only got longer, the truck drivers were instructed to turn around and go back without unloading or loading the merchandise they were supposed to transport.

While all this was happening, Maersk's IT teams found backups of the organization's data. The data was backed up just a couple of days earlier, and for a minute, it seemed Maersk could resume operations very soon. However, to rebuild Maersk's extensive network (45,000 computers and 4,000 servers), they needed

Scams, Hacking, and Cybersecurity

one critical component: a copy of the network topology from the Domain controller servers. Maersk's network used dozens of domain controller servers, to each of which they had backed up the organizational data. The logic behind this network topology was redundancy: if a domain controller server is damaged or fails, another one can take its place with minimal to no downtime. It was almost a perfect backup strategy. However, it failed to consider one edge case: an event that disables all the domain controllers at the same time. And this is exactly what happened here.

No one thought to back up a domain controller; without a domain controller there was no way to restore the data.

> **!** *Sometimes an inch of luck is better than miles of knowledge.*

Shortly before the NotPetya ransomware hit Maersk's global network, one of the company's locations in Ghana, Africa, went offline due to a power outage. Before power was restored, the branch received a message not to go back online because a ransomware attack compromised the network. That was how a remote branch in a small African country ended up having the only working copy of Maersk's entire network topology.

Maersk quickly dispatched someone to retrieve the hard drive from the server and deliver it to the company's IT headquarters in the UK. There, IT teams from all over the world worked diligently to restore the data. Within ten days, Maersk managed to restore some of its computer system and resumed operation, while the full restoration took two months of hard work.

As a result of the ransomware attack, Maersk incurred heavy losses estimated at $200M-300M. The company used the incident to rebuild its network with extensive security, backup, and update measures.

One of the reasons Maersk was able to recover from the incident is its size, strength, and because it's a worldwide global corporation. A smaller company likely wouldn't have survived the incident.

You may have noticed the attackers asked for $300 in ransom, which after multiplying by the number of infected computers, would have cost the company $15M to unlock the data, or 5% of the total losses caused by the cyberattack.

Why didn't Maersk just pay the ransom? Because in this particular case it wouldn't have helped.

Let me explain.

It should be noted that unlike other ransomware, used to extort money from victims, NotPetya was designed primarily to disrupt the organizational operation. Paying the ransom wouldn't have helped in the case of NotPetya because the malware didn't just encrypt the data but also infected the Master Boot Record of the computer, preventing any access to the operating system. If Maersk had tried to pay the ransom, it wouldn't have mattered. They wouldn't have regained access to their data and would have still needed to rebuild their network and restore the data.

NotPetya resulted in a total of $10B in damages worldwide, and to this day is one of the most devastating cyberattacks in history.

Many members of the global cyber community referred to the NotPetya attack as an act of war by Russia against Ukraine. The cyberattack hit four hospitals, two airports, over 20 banks, and

Scams, Hacking, and Cybersecurity

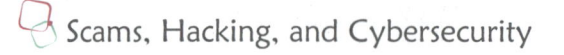

many more organizations. The people of Ukraine discovered that their credit cards stopped working and that they couldn't withdraw money. The attack targeted Ukraine and demonstrated that cyberwars were on the rise and real.

Food for thought:

For many years, people have suspected that government agencies use popular video games and social media platform to collect data. Some argue that Tetris is used by Russia, Angry Birds by the USA, and TikTok – by the Chinese. All to collect personal data for future use.

Ransomware Incident

WannaCry — the Global Angle

NotPetya's impact was clearly global, but I covered it from an organizational angle. The WannaCry incident was different.

At noon on May 12, 2017, I finished giving a college lecture, and headed home. At home, I decided to take a well-deserved nap, and just wanted to check my WhatsApp first. I was bombarded by hundreds of unread messages on professional WhatsApp groups.

Soon afterwards, I learned that a large-scale ransomware attack took place and was quickly propagating throughout Europe.

My cyber community colleagues and I closely followed the reports that day and learned that the ransomware was exploiting a known vulnerability that could be patched. I immediately contacted the IT team of the organization I was working for at the time, explained

Scams, Hacking, and Cybersecurity

the situation, and we made sure all our systems were up to date and protected against this ransomware.

While I was somewhat calm because I knew the organization I was working for was safe, more and more reports surfaced about the global impact of the ransomware attack.

Within hours, reports of more victims started to surface: a Spanish telephone operator, Deutsche Bahn, FedEx, and the National Health Service (NHS) in the UK were significantly hit, so much so that Theresa May, the then Prime Minister of the UK, issued a statement admitting that while that attack didn't target the NHS specifically, the NHS was hit considerably nonetheless. Appointments and operations were cancelled or relocated to different clinics because the attack brought some hospitals and clinics to a standstill.

At the same time, British computer security researcher Marcus Hutchins found a copy of the ransomware and started reconstructing the malware in the lab. Hutchins discovered something interesting. Every time the ransomware infected a new computer, it pinged a nonexistent domain address. Hutchins looked up who owned the domain name, and to his surprise he discovered the domain name was available for registration. Marcus registered the domain name and uploaded it. He then ran the ransomware, and when it received a reply from that website, it destroyed itself. Marcuse uncovered the ransomware's hidden kill switch.

This finding stopped the ransomware from spreading further, but the damage was already done. The NHS reported losses of over 90,000,000 GBP due to the attack, and worldwide over 230,000 computers were infected. However, those who tried to pay the ransom never received the decryption key, warning other

Scams, Hacking, and Cybersecurity

victims not to pay the ransom. Resulting in the attackers receiving only $130,000 worth of cryptocurrency in ransom payments, a relatively low amount for such a widespread attack.

You must be wondering why the ransomware had a kill switch? And why didn't the attackers register the kill switch domain name?

The answer to the first question is that a kill switch is a common practice among hackers. One reason for introducing a kill switch is that hackers want control over how and where malware runs. Some types of malware can recognize if they're running on a real production device or in a virtual environment in a security lab. The attackers also want to be able to stop the attack in case it gets out of control or for any other reason.

But why did the attackers fail to register the kill switch domain? I don't have a good answer to this question perhaps they were just careless and lazy.

The attack utilized the EternalBlue exploit, leaked from the NSA by attack group - ShadowBrokers several months before the attack. The exploit took advantage of a known vulnerability in Microsoft's SMB protocol. Though Microsoft issues a security patch against the vulnerability in February 2017, many remined unpatched, and thus, unprotected.

Following the attack, Microsoft issued a special security patch for Windows XP that, despite being unsupported at that time, was still widely used worldwide.

In December 2017, after further investigation into the malware and how it spread, the US government concluded the attack originated from North Korea, an impoverished and isolated country known for its use of ransomware attacks for financial gain.

I consider WannaCry a global ransomware attack for its impact on the public all ver the world.

The NHS was almost brought to a standstill due to this random malware attack. The result significantly impacted public health, and the most worrying aspect perhaps, was that it wasn't a targeted attack. For this reason, we should all be concerned about future attacks, even if we're unlikely to be targeted.

In conclusion: why do we lo se data?

Scams, Hacking, and Cybersecurity

The problem: we lose data

Devices get Stolen

Devices get Broken

Devices get Attacked

Devices get Lost

The Solution: Backup your data!

Scams, Hacking, and Cybersecurity

The easiest way to ensure data availability is setting up a backup routine.

One can backup important data to flash drive, backup computer data to an external hard drive, or sync the data to a cloud service.

The most important part is to select a backup device and strategy that suit your needs.

It's easier than you might think. For details, please refer to the Backups chapter.

Risk Management

In the first half of this book, I covered the risks, threats, and even some of the consequences and implications of cyberattacks and incidents. So far, I've tried to provide you with practical advice and tools to help you minimize the risk and stay safe online. However, before diving into security tools and how to use them, one must first understand the concept of risk management and how to use it to select the appropriate security tools for your need.

Risk management includes more than information security. Risk management is used by bankers when they review investment opportunities, by insurance companies to determine the insurance premium, and by organizations to assess operational risks, such as considering environmental and political risks when selecting a new office location. We all use risk management daily when making decisions, such as whether to get baggage insurance before the next vacation abroad, should I get a flu vaccine, when to leave for a meeting, and many more decisions.

Scams, Hacking, and Cybersecurity

In the world of organizational information security, risk management is the basis of any plan or project.

When an information security manager reviews the organization's security measures, they must consider the risks, threats, and attack surface to which the organization is exposed.

We all engage in risk management every day, even if only unwittingly. In this chapter, I'll present the main principles of risk management, which you can implement in your daily routine to improve decisions related to information security.

Examples:

When choosing a location for a new office, the risks associated with the work environment are an important consideration. Should you lease an office space downtown or in a less congested area? Should it be located next to a major road? And so on. Apart from operational risks, information security threats and risks should also be considered. For example: if the new office is in Florida, there's a greater risk of a hurricane, and the appropriate measures should be taken to ensure data availability. Conversely, if the office is in Tel Aviv, the risk of a hurricane is practically non-existent, but there's a greater risk of war or missile attack.

Regarding the technical element, the risk profile is even easier to determine. Supposed a significant vulnerability was discovered in Windows, but your organization is using Mac computers. In that case, the vulnerability is irrelevant to the operation environment, and therefore no need to take any action.

Any risk management process begins with identifying the risk and the damage that risk could cause.

The risk assessment can be:

- Quantitative: if X occurs it will cost Y;

  or

- Qualitative, if X occurs the damage level will be low, moderate, or high[15].

Usually, it's very difficult to accurately quantify the damage. For example:

Imagine that your computer was hit by ransomware, and you've backed up your data seven days ago. You wipe the disk and restore the data from backup. What did you actually lose? A day of work, which was the time you spent wiping the drive and restoring the data, and the files you worked on during the past week and didn't backup. But what's the cost? How valuable were the files? Will you be able to restore the data? What happened because you were unavailable today? Maybe you had a critical engagement you couldn't attend or maybe it was just your typical Tuesday.

Now, extrapolate these questions to organizations with dozens and hundreds of users, and I'm sure you'll understand why quantitative evaluation is so challenging.

However, while qualitative evaluation is more intuitive and less accurate, it does provide a quick overview of the risk profile using a scale, in our example of three risk levels: low, moderate, and high.

When an organization ranks the risks using this scale, the major and minor risks quickly become evident.

---

[15] Every organization uses a different risk assessment scale, it could be Low, Medium, High; Low, Medium, High, Critical, 1-5, 1-7, or any other scale the organization deems appropriate.

Scams, Hacking, and Cybersecurity

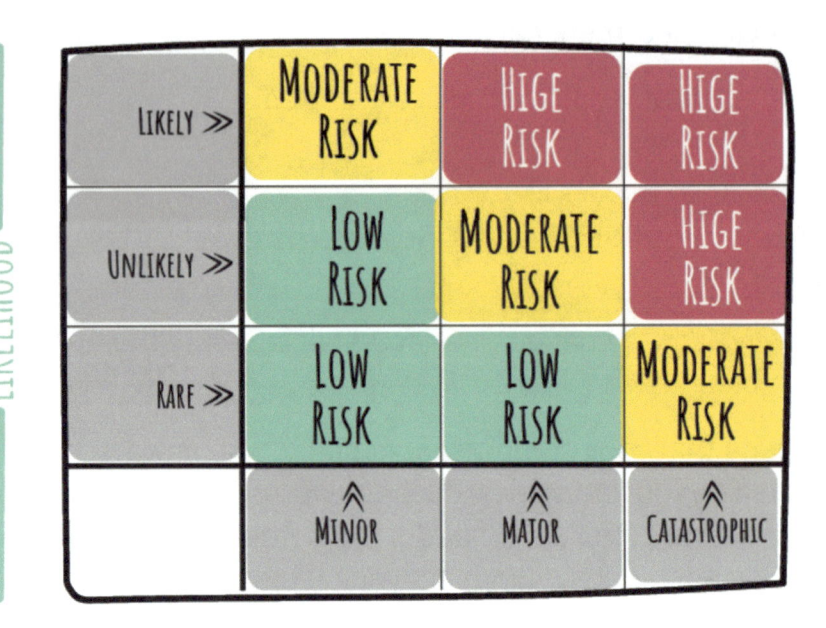

	MINOR	MAJOR	CATASTROPHIC
LIKELY »	MODERATE RISK	HIGE RISK	HIGE RISK
UNLIKELY »	LOW RISK	MODERATE RISK	HIGE RISK
RARE »	LOW RISK	LOW RISK	MODERATE RISK

LIKELIHOOD / CONSEQUENCES

This risk chart allows the information security manager to assess whether the security measures the organization uses are fit for purpose and then to decide which measures to use and when.

But how do you perform personal risk management? Basically, the same way as organizations manage them: you start by identifying the assets you wish to protect.

The first step of any risk management process — whether for an organization or personal — is mapping the assets. An asset is anything you consider valuable. The value can be tangible, that is has a finite monetary value, such as a financial resource or the cost of hardware or software; or intangible such as data, photos, or reputation:

The following questions will help you identify and quantify your assets:

How many computers and mobile devices do I own?

What kind of operating system does each device use?

What data is important to you?

Where is this data stored?

Who uses the data?

How frequently is the data updated?

What are the consequences of data corruption?

- *Leaks to unauthorized parties — a confidentiality breach?*
- *Changes without your knowledge or control — failure of data integrity?*

   or

- *Becomes inaccessible — data availability breach failure.*

The risk management process doesn't have to be long or complicated, but I strongly recommend creating a new spreadsheet, write down all your assets, and spend some time reviewing it to make sure nothing is amiss.

The assets list makes it easier to understand the risks and damage associated with each asset and what security measures are most appropriate.

Practical Security Tools and Techniques

Based on the security incidents I've reviewed so far, I've put together a list of practical tools and techniques for online safety. These include quick and simple methods for detecting phishing attempts, the importance of using strong passwords, and backing up your data. In this chapter I'll provide an in-depth review of the most important tools and techniques you should adopt.

To make those tools and techniques more accessible, I created a website[16] with detailed guides for each tool or technique, as well as other helpful resources and aids.

---

[16] https://www.maybrooks.net/guidebooks

Scams, Hacking, and Cybersecurity

Guidebooks

Awareness

In a world where most information security events exploit the human element, simply being aware of the risk, already makes you less vulnerable. Awareness is the best line of defense. Awareness means reading email messages with attention to details, being more cautious when using your phone, and generally being more alert to your surroundings.

Detecting Phishing Attacks

When you receive an email, first, look for any red flags.

Scams, Hacking, and Cybersecurity

Phishing red flags

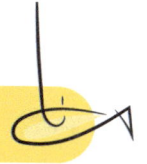

Did you expect this email?

Do you know the sender?

Does the message contain a call to action (download a file \ click a link \ fill in a form)

Is the message random (dear customer, hello)

Does the message contain a link?

Think Before You CLICK

Scams, Hacking, and Cybersecurity

Detecting Vishing Attacks

When you receive an unexpected phone call from a service provider, tell the person on the other side of the line "I'll call you back" and hang up. Even if the person on the other side gave you a few identifying details.

The best protection against vishing calls is to be proactive and call the service provider yourself to verify they have indeed called you.

Before calling back, check the phone number on the service providers' webpage.

General Awareness Tips

Have you received tempting offers and deals before Black Friday? Or a "Special back to school" deal? Hackers customize their attacks just like marketing executives. If you receive an offer that seems too good to be true, it probably is.

! *There's no such thing as a FREE gift*

Scams, Hacking, and Cybersecurity

⚠️ BE EXTRA CAUTIOUS OF TEMPTING EMAILS

Using Encryption

Encryption sounds like a big scary techy word, which usually makes people think it's too complicated for them, but the truth is that we can all use an encryption tool to protect our valuable data.

I promise that after reading this section, using encryption won't seem such a daunting task.

Let's start by explaining the purpose of encryption. The purpose of data encryption is to protect the data's confidentiality and in certain cases, integrity. It's important to choose an encryption method that suits your needs.

Scams, Hacking, and Cybersecurity

Most of us use encryptions without even realizing it. Every time you visit a website using the HTTPS protocol, recognizable by the URL beginning with https:// instead of http:// and the padlock symbol (for more details, see the Safe Browsing chapter), you are in fact using encryption. You've probably also seen the end-to-end encryption message when you've texted someone on WhatsApp. The traffic is encrypted to prevent unauthorized parties from reading your personal communications. The same is true when you protect a Word file using a password. These are all everyday examples of using encryption.

Encryption is reversible by definition. For example, this book was sent to a focus group prior to publication. How did I secure the data to maintain confidentiality? I encrypted the manuscript and emailed it to the focus group members. Then, I sent the password for opening the file to the focus group via a secure messaging app, such as WhatsApp. It's very important to send the encrypted data and decryption key (in this case, a password) separately, because if you accidentally send the data to the wrong person, they will be able to access the encrypted data.

A Brief History

Encryption tools have been in use since the dawn of history.

One of the most ancient encryption methods is Atbash cipher. In Atbash cipher, the first (e.g., A) letter of the Alphabet is replaced by the last (e.g. Z), the second letter (e.g. B) is replaced by the second to last (e.g. Y), and so on. The name Atbash comes from the Hebrew alphabet, in which the first letter – Alef, is replaced by the last letter – Taf, and the second letter – Bet, is replaced by the second to last – Shin.

Scams, Hacking, and Cybersecurity

A	B	C	D	E	F	G	H	I	J	K	L	M	N	O	P	Q	R	S	T	U	V	W	X	Y	Z
Z	Y	X	W	V	U	T	S	R	Q	P	O	N	M	L	K	J	I	H	G	F	E	D	C	B	A

Atbash cipher

In ancient Rome, military communications were encrypted using the Caesar cipher, named after Julius Caesar. It was a simple substitution cipher that used a wheel with two sets of alphabets. A key was selected for each message, indicating the alphabet shift: the number of positions each letter of the text has been moved. For example, when using a shift of four A is replaced with E; B is replaced with F; and so on. Knowing the alphabet shift is the key to decoding the message.

Caesar Cipher (alphabet shift).

Scams, Hacking, and Cybersecurity

> Teach your children Atbash cipher and start communicating in encrypted messages.

The early 20th century marked the beginning of the modern cryptography era. Using mechanical, and later digital, devices enabled the development of much more sophisticated encryption techniques. The Enigma machine in WWII is probably the best-known example signifying the transition into the modern cryptography era. The machine was developed in 1918 and was initially sold to the commercial market. However, it was later used by the German navy and army, improving the cipher and turning the machine into the main encryption device used throughout World War II.

Since then, encryption techniques became ubiquitous, so much so, that today anyone who uses the internet is using some form of encryption, albeit usually unknowingly.

Key Encryption Terminology

Plaintext: the unencrypted data we want to encrypt.

Ciphertext: the plaintext data after it was encrypted. Encrypted data cannot be read without a decryption key.

Encryption: the process of converting plaintext into ciphertext

Decryption: the process of converting ciphertext into its original plaintext form.

Symmetric encryption: using the same key for encrypting and decrypting the data.

Asymmetric encryption: using a pair of related keys — one public and the other private — to encrypt and decrypt the data. The private key is a secret, whereas the public key is known to everyone.

If Alice (A) wants to send an encrypted message to Bob (B) using asymmetric encryption, she can use Bob's **public key**. The only way to decrypt the message is by using the related **private key** that only Bob has. Asymmetric encryption is often used for sharing symmetrical encryption keys securely. This is an example of using asymmetric encryption for maintaining confidentiality. But there are other things that can be achieved by using such algorithms. For example, if the roles of the public and private keys will be reversed. The Senders' private key will encrypt the data, that can be opened by anyone, as everyone has access to the related public key. In this example the encryption is used for proof of origin.

Hash: Hashing is a hybrid element in cryptography. Unlike most encryption techniques that are two-way functions: **Plaintext > Encrypted text > Plaintext**, hashing is a one-way function used to verify the integrity of the data. This means that a hash function is irreversible and there is no way of retrieving the Plaintext from the hash.

A hash function takes your plaintext and generates an output of a fixed length, which serves as the digital signature of the data. Regardless of whether the text consists of 3 pages or 300 pages, the length of the hash value is the same. Any change to the text, even the smallest, will change the hash value. Therefore, a hash function is typically used to verify that the data hasn't changed, or in other words: to verify the integrity of the data.

Encrypting Personal Data

As I've mentioned, most users aren't aware they're using encryption each and every single day. When you visit a secured website, save a password on your browser or connect to the office from your laptop through a VPN; you're using encryption!

Encrypting Sensitive Information:

The most common use of encryption in our day-to-day lives is securing sensitive information. Current versions of the MS Office suite allow you to protect a file with a password. Unfortunately, many people aren't aware of this option, and continue to send sensitive information as plaintext. I believe that if you've reached this chapter, by now, you recognize the risks and why we need to be more careful when sharing our information.

To password protect an MS Office file (Word, Excel, PowerPoint), open the file, click on File -> Info -> click on the Protect Document button and choose your password. I strongly advise doing this before sharing any personal or business sensitive information with someone.

You should then send the password separately via a text message, WhatsApp, or even on a phone call.

Another common use of encryption is encrypting entire folders before sending them to someone or copying them to an external storage device, for example via the popular 7ZIP file archiver tool.

Scams, Hacking, and Cybersecurity

> **!** *Important: decrypting encrypted files or folders is impossible to do without the password. Make sure you remember the encryption password.*

Full Disk Encryption:

Losing a mobile device is frustrating. After buying a new device, you need to restore all your data. Losing a device is frustrating enough without having to worry about losing sensitive data.

There's a wide selection of encryption solutions, including BitLocker (the included encryption feature in the Pro and Enterprise versions of Windows).

Password Management

The average person has 20 to 30 online accounts. Sounds like too much? Let's review:

Scams, Hacking, and Cybersecurity

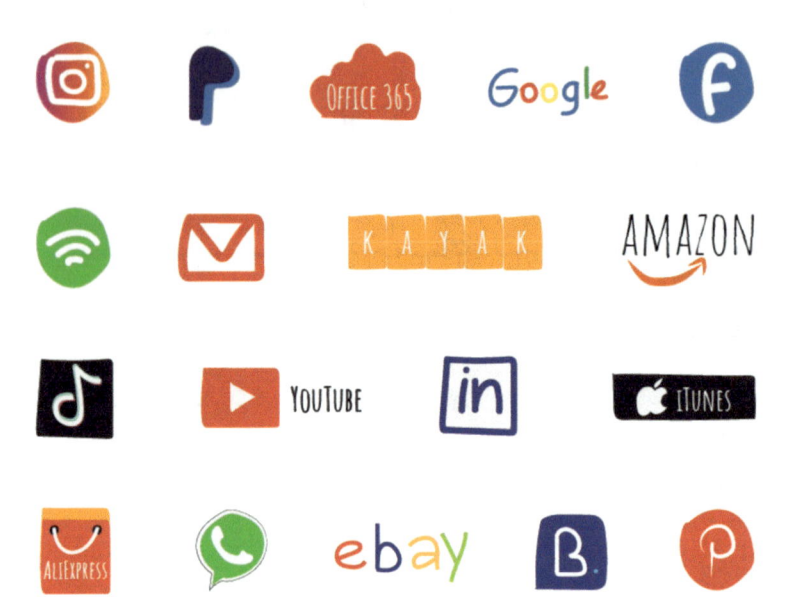

Most of us have more than one email address, more than one online banking account, accounts at several online shopping websites, multiple social media accounts, not to mention passwords you use to log into your computer, smartphone, and tablet.

Logically speaking, this is where I should have advised you to use a unique and different password for each account, but even I, who's obsessed with cybersecurity practices, fully admit it isn't practical. According to a study conducted by Google in 2019, 66% of Americans reuse the same password for several accounts, and the other 44% are probably using a password management tool. This comes as no surprise. Our minds aren't good at remembering random combinations of letters and numbers, especially if we've chosen a long and complex password; but more on that shortly. In the "Data Confidentiality Breach" chapter I described how attackers use leaked passwords to hijack sensitive accounts and use them to increase the credibility of their social engineering attacks.

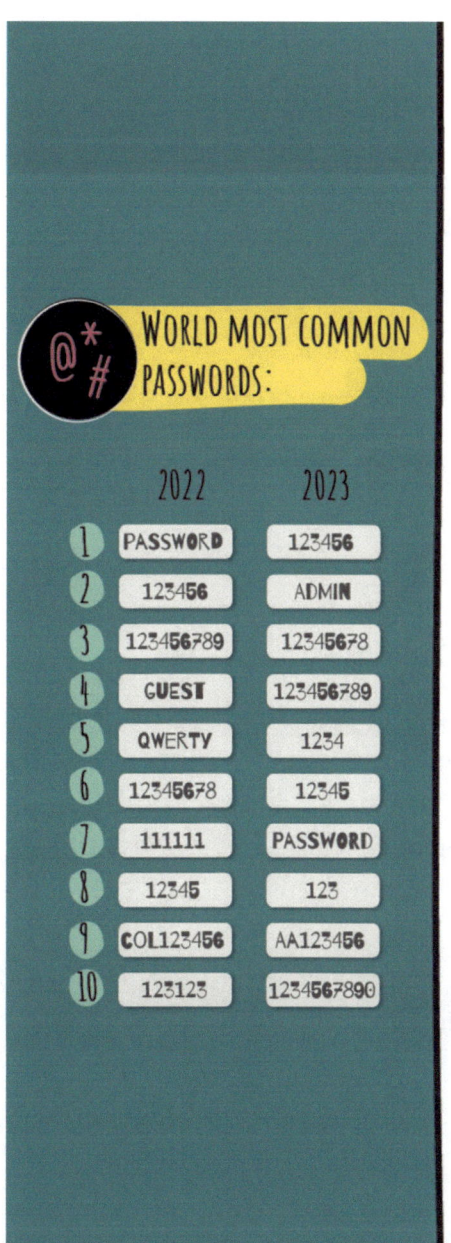

Scams, Hacking, and Cybersecurity

World Most Common Passwords:

#	2022	2023
1	PASSWORD	123456
2	123456	ADMIN
3	123456789	12345678
4	GUEST	123456789
5	QWERTY	1234
6	12345678	12345
7	111111	PASSWORD
8	12345	123
9	COL123456	AA123456
10	123123	1234567890

40% of Americans had their personal data leaked

66%% of Americans reuse their password in multiple accounts

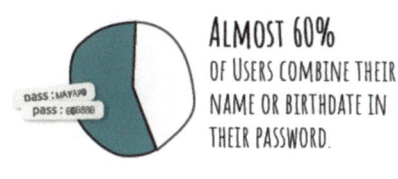

Almost 60% of users combine their name or birthdate in their password.

Over 50% of users share their password with their Spouse

Only 11% of users change their password after a breakup

Scams, Hacking, and Cybersecurity

Google's full report and other similar reports paint a worrisome picture.

Password Threats

A brute force attack is a cyberattack in which the attacker attempts to guess the password. The attacker uses long and extensive precomputed tables, including:

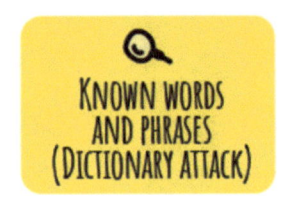

- **COMMON PASSWORDS** (123456)
- **KNOWN WORDS AND PHRASES (DICTIONARY ATTACK)**
- **LEAKED PASSWORDS**

Rainbow tables. Sounds harmless, right?

Not quite. Rainbow tables contain large quantities of password hashes (for more details, please see Hash in the Encryption chapter). Rainbow tables have significantly improved the efficiency of a brute force attack. Sending the hash values to a central database is much quicker than sending the actual passwords.

How does one run such an attack? It's quite easy. There are free, though a bit shady, programs that will run the attack for you. All you have to do is sit back and wait patiently. Of course, the free password cracking tools are less likely to prove useful the more complex the password.

Choosing a Strong Password

As a rule of thumb: the longer the password, the longer it will take to crack it. It's a matter of statistical probability. A longer password means more options must be checked until the right password is found.

In the past, 4-character long passwords were very common and even recommended. However, as processing power continued to increase so did the requirement for longer passwords. And so, 4-character passwords turned into 6-character passwords in 00s, then 7 characters, 8 characters, and currently the recommended password length is 12 characters, although if the password is sufficiently complex, 8 characters might do.

The password length isn't the only important parameter. The current characteristics of strong passwords are:

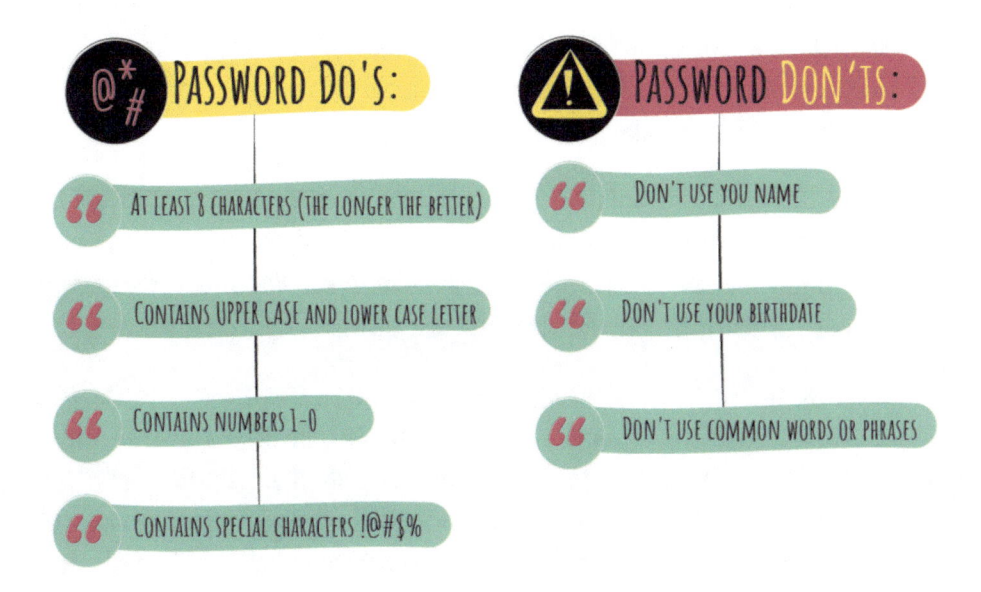

Password Do's:
- At least 8 characters (the longer the better)
- Contains upper case and lower case letter
- Contains numbers 1-0
- Contains special characters !@#$%

Password Don'ts:
- Don't use you name
- Don't use your birthdate
- Don't use common words or phrases

Scams, Hacking, and Cybersecurity

Following these guidelines, a good password should look something like T%dw/3B). But who can remember it? This is why we developed techniques for generating easier to remember passwords.

> *Ready for a challenge? Open Google 'Password Generator' and try to memorize the generated passwords.*

Tips for Selecting a Strong Password

- Using a passphrase: a sentence-like string of words that is longer than a traditional password, easier to remember and more difficult to crack. For example: 'LittleREDridinghood1!'. Word of caution – it's better to use a phrase that means something to you, but isn't too common, e.g., a sentence from a song you like.

- Mnemonic password: using a memorable phrase and using it in the password. If I like the Beatles, I might choose 'All you need is love' as my password: *AllYoUNeEdISlOVe!*. It's easier to remember, but difficult to crack using a brute force attack.

- Speak more than one language? That's an advantage. You can type the password in one language, Hebrew in my case, only using English letters. For example, if I type the phrase StrongPassword1@ in Hebrew, but use the English keyboard instead, I end up with the password Xhxnvjzev1@. It's a phrase I can easily remember, but in English it's nothing more than a string of random letters, numbers, and special characters.

Scams, Hacking, and Cybersecurity

?

Do you want to test if your password is strong enough?

Google 'Password Strength Check' and test your password is.

But remember – never use your actual password, just something similar!

> **TREAT YOUR PASSWORD IS LIKE A TOOTHBRUSH:**
> * PICK A GOOD ONE
> * CHANGE FREQUENTLY
> * DON'T SHARE IT WITH OTHERS

How to Remember These Strong Passwords

You've chosen a strong password. Now what? Should you choose such a password to each account you use? How can you remember all those unique and strong passwords for your dozens and dozens of online accounts? Does it even make sense to try? I don't think so. So, what's the solution?

The main purpose of this book is to provide you with **practical** tools and actionable advice. I admit that I'm only human, and I don't use a unique password for each and every online account. However, I must stress that I don't reuse the same password everywhere. I have a number of passwords that I use according to the sensitivity of the data:

- Finances (bank, credit card, PayPal).
- Sensitive personal information (healthcare services provider, government agencies, insurance).
- Personal (social media, online shopping, travel apps).
- Business (email, company data, client data, professional websites).

All my passwords are very strong regardless of the data's sensitivity, because I consider all data sensitive and I never mix the above categories. It's important to note that I don't use the same password in each category, I just use the same convention, so all my financial passwords will have the same structure, but each is unique. This is also how I remember the passwords. When I log in to my online banking account, I know to use my financial services password convention + the unique identifier for this service.

How do I remember all those passwords?

1. I use naming conventions: over the years I have developed a couple of mnemonic devices that help me remember the naming conventions. I use these to generate similar but different passwords for each data sensitivity category and for each service.

2. Changing passwords: since I know that reusing passwords is not ideal, I replace them at least once every 3 months. Changing a password doesn't necessarily mean generating a completely new password. Replacing a few characters is generally enough. For example: adding a number at the beginning or end of the password, changing the uppercase and lowercase letters, and similar substitutions are enough to confuse most password verification tools and more importantly – leaked password databases.

3. Logging in to online accounts using Google, Facebook, and similar services, is very convenient and I often use this option. However, it also means that my Google and Facebook passwords become a critical point of failure, which is why I use complex passwords and change them frequently, and, naturally, enable multi-factor authentication, everywhere I can (more on this in the next section). Putting all your eggs in one basket is risky, we can use this as a risk management exercise, taking into account how secure the basket is, the convenience, easy-to-remember passwords, and general ease of use and do they outweigh the potential risk.

What about password managers?

There are plenty of password management tools available on the market today. Some of them are completely free, while others use a Freemium pricing model (basic features for free, additional features at a cost).

! *Password managers are excellent tools, as long as you don't forget the master password.*

Scams, Hacking, and Cybersecurity

Despite their flaws, password managers can prevent common mistakes, thereby enhancing information security. Most password managers ask you to enter a master password, which is a long and complex password used to access your other passwords, and then will automatically fill your login credentials on all websites.

One of Google Chrome's features is a built-in password manager. Google's password manager isn't as advanced as the paid password managers that offer advanced features such as encrypted file storage, but it has all the basic features most users need.

In late 2019, Google updated its password manager, adding new features, including reused password warning, alerts for leaked passwords, and a random password generator.

Because most people use Google's ecosystem and Chrome as their browser, this is definitely a tool worth knowing.

Word of caution – if you use a shared device, it's crucial to log out of your google account if you use it to store your passwords.

There are various password management tools you can use to protect your accounts and those of your loved ones (e.g. LastPass, 1Password, Nord and more). Some of these tools are free while others offer a more robust protection suite usually at a cost.

Personally, I'm not too keen on password managers. *The chain is only as strong as the weakest link*, and unfortunately some password managers were hacked before. If you do use a password manager, I would advise not to use it for EVERYTHING. Keep your most important accounts to yourself.

Important tip: the master password to your password manager is the key to your kingdom. The master password should be strong and use multi-factor authentication (MFA).

What about writing down the password on a piece of paper?

Many people still write down their passwords on post-its and then stick them on their computer or hide them under the keyboard. This is a security breach waiting to happen. Writing your passwords on post-its opens your information or your organization to a potential data breach as someone is likely to get a hold of them sooner or later. Also, it's difficult keeping the notes up to date. I met someone who wrote down all her passwords in a notebook. Every time she updated a password, she needed to update the entire notebook. This is not practical in the long-term.

If you find it difficult to remember passwords, it's better to write them in a secure note-taking app on your phone instead of using a post-it that could easily fall into the wrong hands. This secure note should be helpful to you but not for a potential attacker, and therefore should include only the list of passwords or hints and not the website URL or your full login credentials.

For more details about password management you can visit the guidebook[17]:

---

[17] https://www.maybrooks.net/passwords

Scams, Hacking, and Cybersecurity

Multi-Factor Authentication (MFA)

MFA is one of the most effective security tools for protecting your personal information online. Multi-factor authentication requires three pieces of evidence to authenticate (called factors):

- Something you know (a password or PIN)
- Something you have (a security token or smartphone)
- Something you are (biometrics)

Today the most common implementation of MFA is 2-factor authentication (2FA): something you know and something you have.

There are many examples of a 2FA process, but the most common one starts with typing in a username and password, and then a one-time code the user receives via a text message, a phone call, an email, an authenticator app, or by using a security token (such as a USB security key).

Scams, Hacking, and Cybersecurity

Many people use 2FA on a daily basis. For example: when you transfer money to someone you are asked to enter a code sent via a text message. But not everyone uses 2FA in their personal life.

We detected an unusual login attempt from Indonesia. Was it you?

These alerts shouldn't be taken lightly. This is an indication the system has detected an unusual login attempt to your account. Most email services and social media platforms track your daily usage patterns and send you a notification if a login attempt was detected from an unusual location or at an unusual time. If I logged into my Facebook account from New York and an hour later another login attempt was recorded from London, this is considered unusual and will trigger a security notification. I've logged into my Facebook account from London many times before, so in itself, this isn't suspicious. But there's no way I could have traveled from New York to London in an hour.

Currently, most websites offer a 2FA. Usually, when you set up the process, it will make you go through a 2FA process each time you login. But as the platform learns your patterns, the 2FA requests will reduce, usually asking you to go through the 2FA process only on new devices or when login attempt is out of usual patterns. I recommend setting up a 2FA for login attempts from new devices, especially on your main email and social media accounts.

Using biometrics (fingerprint, face recognition) is considered a very secure form of MFA because it's almost forgery-proof.

Scams, Hacking, and Cybersecurity

How 2FA works:

- Upon login you'll be asked to add a onetime code
- The code is sent via text message or generated on app
- Enter the code and log in

Where should you set 2FA:

(Facebook, Instagram, Email, Office 365)

For more details about multi-factor authentication please visit the guide[18]:

---
[18] https://www.maybrooks.net/mfa

Scams, Hacking, and Cybersecurity

Safe Browsing

Every time we do something online, we leave a trail of digital breadcrumbs that reveal the sites we've visited, our interests, health issues, our dream vacation destination, our favorite cuisine, and so much more. Your country and foreign governments, advertisement companies, and social media companies use these breadcrumbs to watch your every move. This tracking has some advantages, but also creates room for concern.

If a person goes missing, a quick review of their browsing history can reveal their potential whereabouts, who they were supposed to meet, and what was their state of mind.

Furthermore, I must admit that I'd rather see targeted ads about a vacation in Thailand than about something I have no interest in whatsoever. Occasionally searching for 'hotels in Thailand' could help search engines display relevant ads that I'm more likely to click on.

But what about privacy? What if I want to browse the web without being watched?

While modern browsers have a private browsing mode, all this feature does is not save the browsing history and local data (cookies) for the current private session. While this can be useful in some cases, a common misconception is that private browsing protects your privacy.

!
> If the product is FREE
>
> The product is YOU!

Scams, Hacking, and Cybersecurity

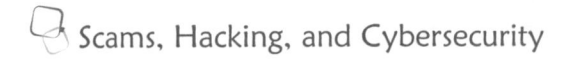

Safe browsing is more than avoiding being watched by governments. Online banking, e-commerce sites, social media platforms and other players have a good reason to know who you are.

Staying anonymous online is virtually impossible. You can get a dedicated computer and a VPN to hide your location. You can start using the TOR browser, the browser used for accessing the dark web, and browse anonymously. However, these measures are impractical and unnecessary for the average user[19].

For most users, however, safe browsing means safely protecting personal information from unauthorized access and using websites such as online banking and other sensitive accounts.

The first thing to verify when visiting such a website is that the website is secure:

---

[19] If you still want to know how to be anonymous on the web, I highly recommend reading the book The Art of Invisibility by Kevin Mitnick.

Scams, Hacking, and Cybersecurity

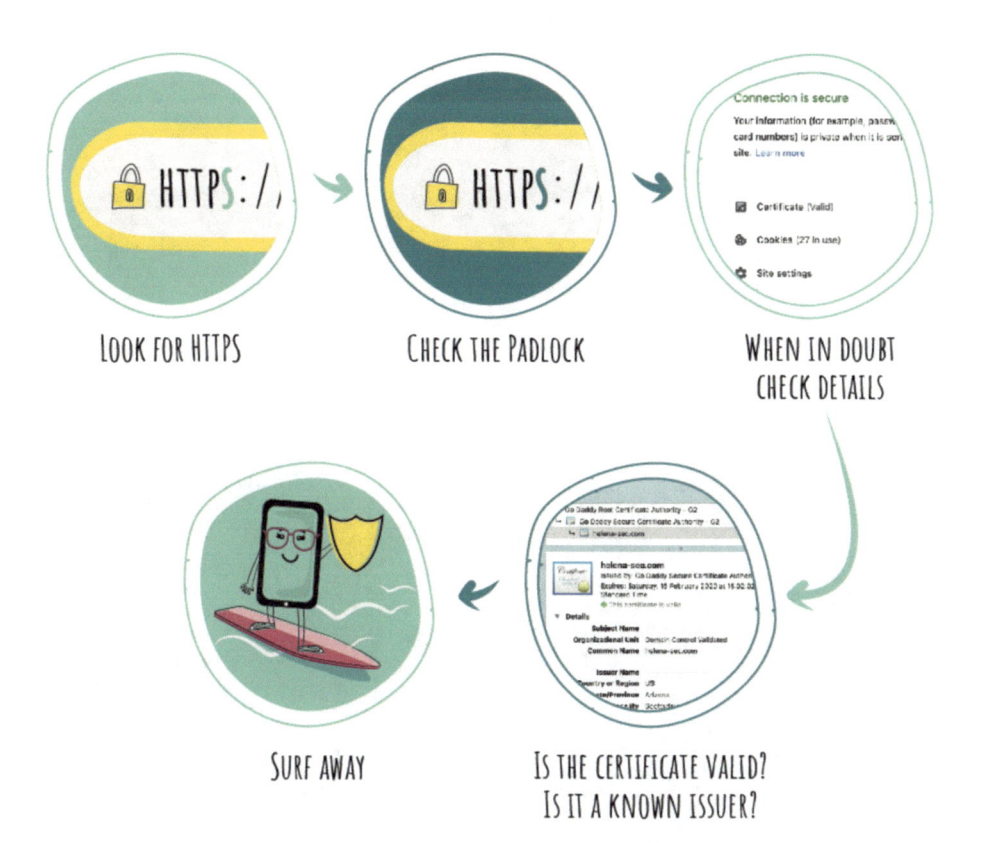

🔒 HTTPS://WWW.How to check if the website your browsing is secured.com 🔍

Look for HTTPS → **Check the Padlock** → **When in doubt check details**

Surf away ← **Is the certificate valid? Is it a known issuer?**

Verifying the website is secure is important, but there are other safe web browsing practices to follow.

Scams, Hacking, and Cybersecurity

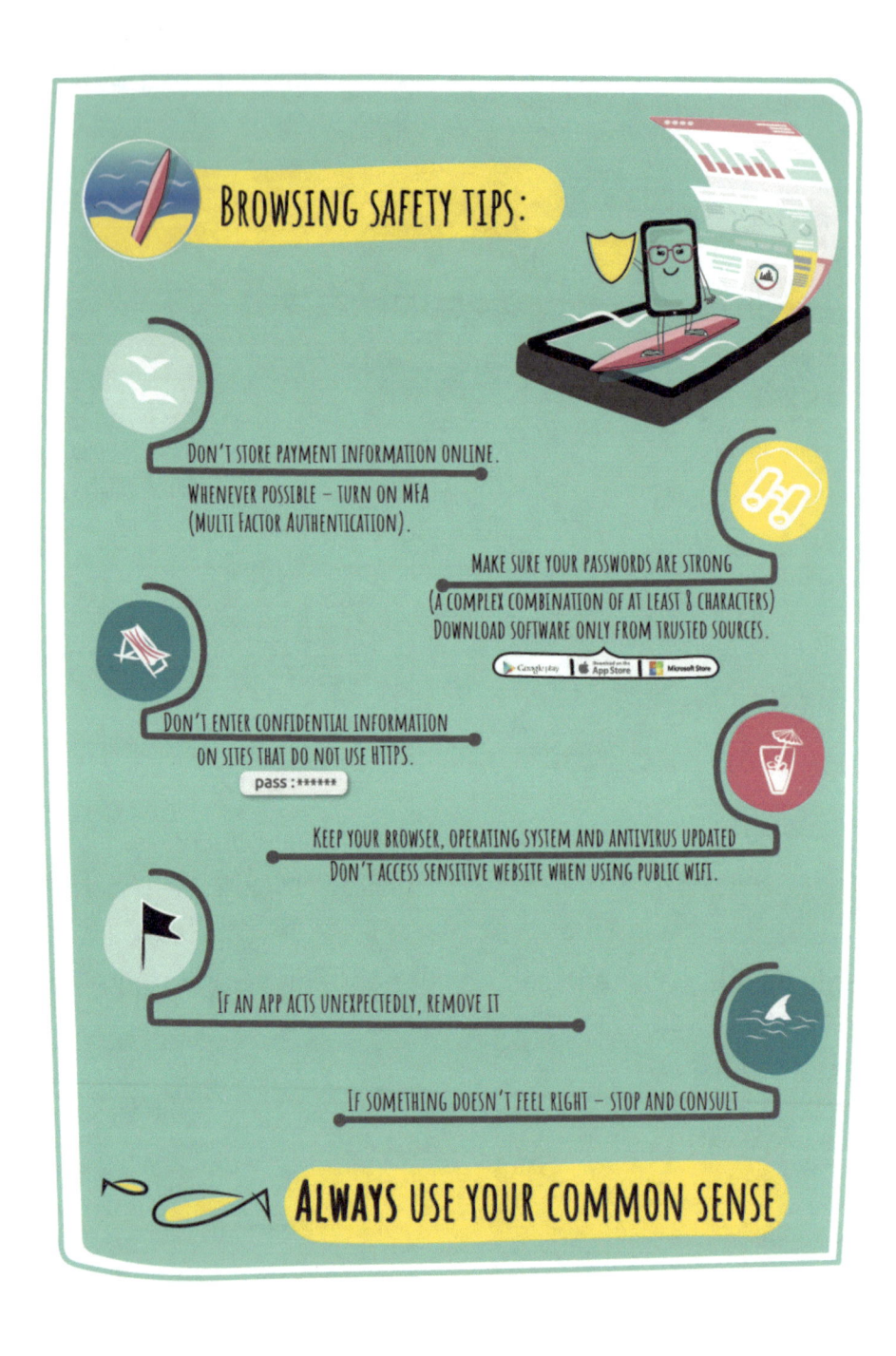

Browsing safety tips:

Don't store payment information online.

Whenever possible – turn on MFA (Multi Factor Authentication).

Make sure your passwords are strong (a complex combination of at least 8 characters)

Download software only from trusted sources.

Don't enter confidential information on sites that do not use HTTPS.

Keep your browser, operating system and antivirus updated

Don't access sensitive website when using public wifi.

If an app acts unexpectedly, remove it

If something doesn't feel right – stop and consult

Always use your common sense

Scams, Hacking, and Cybersecurity

Using Public Wi-Fi

In the past, the only way to connect to the internet on-the-go or in a meeting outside the office was by using an expensive cellular modem. Then, Internet cafés providing their customers with internet access became very popular. Today, free public Wi-Fi is common in many businesses and venues: restaurants, cafés, gas stations, shopping centers, airports, hotels, and even citywide. While very convenient, public Wi-Fi isn't very secure. Wireless networks are vulnerable to all sorts of attacks and they must be secured to be safe. Unfortunately, many public wireless networks are not secure enough and, therefore, unsafe.

An attacker connected to a public Wi-Fi puts all other network users at risk. I would encourage you to refrain from using public Wi-Fi, and if you must, then avoid surfing to sensitive sites like online banking or similar sensitive online accounts. It is advised to use a VPN when connecting to a public Wi-Fi, so if you travel a lot and prefer using a public Wi-Fi connection, it's a good idea to invest in a VPN account.

With cellular data plans having more bandwidth and becoming more affordable, I recommend using your phone as a mobile hotspot for your computer and other devices instead of using public Wi-Fi. If you can't use your phone as a mobile hotspot, wait until you can connect to a private network before accessing any sensitive online accounts.

You can detect a data leak or malicious code running on your computer by opening your Task Manager and checking which processes are transmitting data over the network. If you close all the programs that require an internet connection, such as web browsers and media players, and there's still network usage, this means that a potentially malicious program might be running in the background.

Scams, Hacking, and Cybersecurity

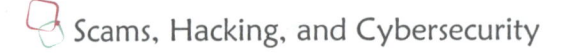

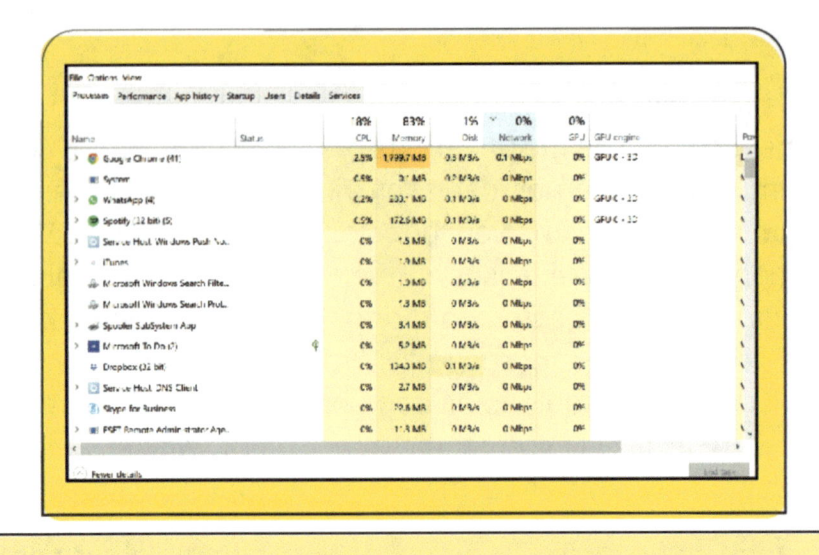

Endpoint Security

Whether your endpoint device is a desktop computer, laptop computer, tablet, or smartphone, securing the device reduces risk and supports safe browsing.

Being smart online and aware of red flags is the most important element in protecting your identity and data, but even the most knowledgeable and vigilant person can fall victim to cyberattacks. Accidently or absentmindedly clicking on a pop-up message, a very convincing phishing email, or connecting an unknown storage device to your computer, could all compromise the device.

As a rule of thumb, endpoint security consists of three layers: protect, prevent, and prepare.

ENDPOINT PROTECTION

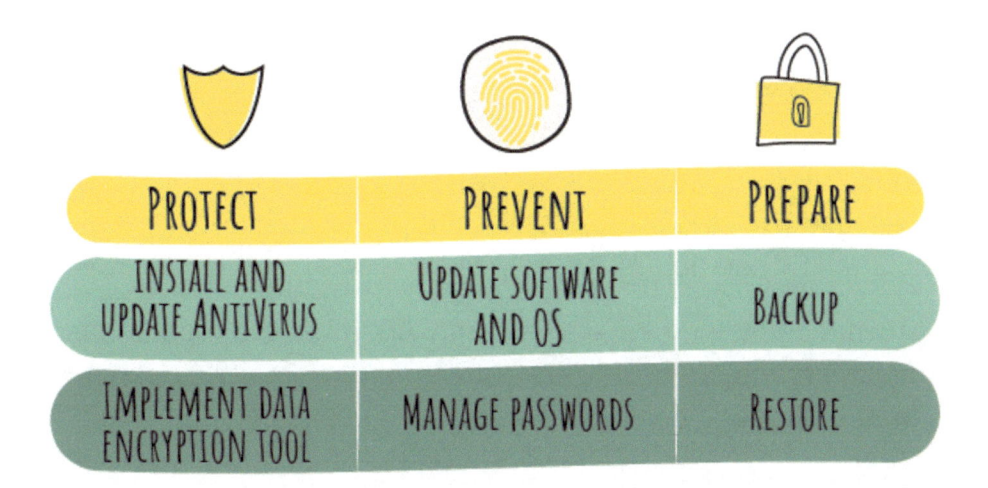

PROTECT	PREVENT	PREPARE
INSTALL AND UPDATE ANTIVIRUS	UPDATE SOFTWARE AND OS	BACKUP
IMPLEMENT DATA ENCRYPTION TOOL	MANAGE PASSWORDS	RESTORE

These three security layers provide continuous endpoint protection. Since new threats always emerge, using an antivirus alone isn't enough. It's also important to keep the operating system and all security software up-to-date, regularly change your passwords, and schedule periodic backups, with a backup interval appropriate for your needs and circumstances. For more details about backups, please refer to the Backups chapter.

Security Updates

After their release, operating systems, programs, and applications get updated, fixed, or improved through software updates. Both hackers and vulnerability researchers, study operating systems, programs, and applications in an attempt to discover vulnerabilities that could be exploited. There are many flaws that can lead to a vulnerability. The main cause for vulnerabilities is flaws in the code. Vulnerability researchers and hackers compete with each other on who will be the first to discover a vulnerability. When hackers discover unknown vulnerabilities, referred to as Zero-day vulnerabilities, as no one, including the vendor, knows about it, they can launch an attack to exploit them. When researchers discover an unknown vulnerability before the hackers do, or before the vulnerability can be exploited, they report it to the developing company. Code flaws leading to vulnerabilities can usually be fixed through a software update. Companies aspire to release updates and patches before the vulnerability can be exploited by bad actors.

Software developers release security updates on a regular basis, and emergency (also called out-of-band) security updates for serious vulnerabilities that must be immediately patched.

In addition to security updates, developers release hotfixes (bug fixes) and new software versions. Developers continue to support older versions until a version reaches its End of Life (EOL) date and becomes discontinued. When a software reaches its End of Life date, active development stops, but continues to receive security updates for a while longer until it reaches its End of Support (EOS) date.

Many users fail to upgrade their operating system and programs before they reach their End of Support date. As a result, many devices continue to run unsupported operating systems that no longer receive security updates. This creates a risk because hackers continue to look for vulnerabilities in outdated operating systems without having to worry about a security patch that might thwart their malicious plans.

Scams, Hacking, and Cybersecurity

This risk materialized in the WannaCry and Not Petya cyberattacks that I had described in detail in the Failure of Data Availability Chapter. Many users continued to use the Windows XP operating system long after it reached its End of Support date back in 2014, three years prior to the attack.

Keeping your security software (e.g. antivirus) up-to-date is just as important. Antivirus software gets updated regularly with signatures of new malware. Therefore, using outdated antivirus software is very risky because the antivirus doesn't protect against newly discovered malware and threats.

Most operating systems and security software support automatic updates, and this is the recommended setting for home users.

If you can't upgrade your operating system because the new version cannot be supported on your old hardware, or you don't have the necessary license, or for any other reason, it's imperative to add additional controls, such as more frequent backups, to compensate for the greater risk, as well as consider upgrading as soon as possible.

For more details about endpoint security, visit the guidebook[20]:

---

[20] https://www.maybrooks.net/homeprotect

Scams, Hacking, and Cybersecurity

Mobile Device Security

Mobile Device Security is a sub-category of endpoint security. Most of us own a smartphone, a laptop, and sometimes a tablet too. Each of these devices forms a potential attack surface. A software environment through which an attacker may obtain unauthorized access to data that attackers can target. While the three layers of endpoint security — protection, prevention, and preparedness — apply to Mobile Device Security as well, there are mobile-specific rules that can reduce mobile risks and threats:

Scams, Hacking, and Cybersecurity

Mobile Device Protection:

Use strong authentication:
Define biometric authentication (fingerprint \ face recognition) for all devices, reducing risk of data leakage if the device is misused.

Protect your device:
Use antivirus and other protection software to reduce risks. Consider adding "remote wipe" protection to your device.

Use Encryption:
If the mobile device holds sensitive data, consider using full disk encryption.

Application:
Install apps from official stores only.

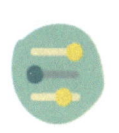

Application permissions:
Give application only necessary and relevant permissions. If the app requires elevates permissions, chose another app (e.g. - flashlight app requesting access to contact list).

Scams, Hacking, and Cybersecurity

Backups:

In the words of Douglas Adams[21]: "Don't panic!" Devising a backup strategy isn't as daunting as it might sound. You'll have to review and adjust your strategy periodically according to the type of data you're using and changing circumstances.

The first step of every backup strategy is answering the question: what data has to be backed up, and for what purpose? The answer to this question will help you determine where to back up, backup frequency, how many devices will be backed up, and how much storage space is required for the backup. These parameters change over time.

As of June 2023, a 5TB external hard drive costs about $100. That is about 15¢ per 1GB of storage. Considering how affordable data storage is, it's almost negligent not to back up data.

---

[21] "The Hitchhiker's Guide to the Galaxy", Wings Books, 1979

Scams, Hacking, and Cybersecurity

How to choose a backup?

- What about my Privacy?
- Where will I put it?
- External Device? / Disk On Key
- What Data do I have?
- Paid Service?
- Use Cloud Backup? (One Drive, Google Drive, Dropbox)
- How will I remember to backup?

As undergrads or graduate students, the most important data is school-related documents. Just imagine getting hit by ransomware the day before your term or research paper is due. The data must be backed up frequently, after any major change, and should include, in the very least, all the data from the current and previous term.

Scams, Hacking, and Cybersecurity

Most of us still have our college or university binders stored in our attic or basement, even though we know we'll probably never use them again. However, if you choose to pay every month for a cloud backup solution, I strongly suggest you occasionally review the backed-up content, to determine if the data is still necessary. After graduation, most people can back up all their school work to an external drive and stop backing up to the cloud.

Individuals can use cloud backup and local backup (external hard drive, flash drive, or Network Attached Storage [NAS]). There are dedicated solutions for small and medium sized businesses, but they're beyond the scope of this book.

When choosing the right solution, you first need to define the backup needs and purpose. This will help you determine whether to go with a cloud or a local backup. Then, you need to choose the right backup solution for your needs:

Scams, Hacking, and Cybersecurity

Chose the right backup:

- When you're **OFFLINE**
- When you have **WHERE** to store the device
- When it's for a **SINGLE** device

- When you're **ONLINE**
- When you need **REMOTE ACCESS**
- When you want to **SYNCHRONIZE** to multiple devices

External Storage Device

- ⊖ Requires self discipline
- ⊕ Self controlled
- Manual
- Cheap
- Simple setting

Cloud Backup

- ⊖ Requires initial settings
- ⊕ Automatic
- Monthly cost
- Accessible from everywhere
- Privacy concerns

Scams, Hacking, and Cybersecurity

When choosing the right backup strategy, you must take the following considerations into account:

- Should the backup include data from multiple devices, such as photos or shared work files, or only from a single device?
- Is the data personal or does it need to be shared with others?
- How frequently will the data be accessed?
- Does the backup need to be accessible?

Of course, you should consider how sensitive or confidential the data is. Are you comfortable uploading it to a cloud service you have limited control over?

Cloud storage is becoming more affordable, but protecting sensitive and confidential information remains a concern.

The most common type of data people want to backup is photos. However, not all photos are born equal. Some random photos you took and sent on WhatsApp are probably not as valuable as photos taken on a once-in-a-lifetime trip. Nevertheless, we take a lot of photos and we want to keep them safe.

What is the difference between backup and synchronization?

Backup means an extra copy of data that can be accessed if the source fails or is lost; The purpose of data synchronization (sync for short) is to maintain data consistency between multiple devices in such a way that a change made to the data on one device is immediately updated on all other devices. Data synchronization is critical to an efficient collaboration between team members, but that is not the only use case. For example, when I was writing this chapter, I was on my office computer. The previous chapter was written on my tablet between meetings, and other parts of this book were written on my smartphone on train rides and short breaks. To ensure I always work on the most current draft, I use a cloud service that syncs the files to all my devices, allowing me to keep working on the book at any time, from anywhere, and on any device.

By the way, after each writing session, I also sent myself the latest copy on email, just as an extra precaution. Naturally, the manuscript was encrypted.

Being a cybersecurity expert comes with inherent paranoia.

However, though syncing is convenient, it isn't backing up. Consider the threat of ransomware. If my laptop was infected by ransomware, the encrypted copy of the data might sync to the cloud and then to all my other devices.

Is there a way to minimize this risk? Typically, cloud syncing services, such as Google's Google Drive, Microsoft's OneDrive, and similar services, have a feature called data versioning. Versioning creates a new copy of the data when changes are made and retains the previous versions for up to 30 days. Taking this measure protects against ransomware attacks and other types of accidental data loss by allowing you to restore a version of the data before it was encrypted or corrupted.

Keeping Physical Backup Media Safe

Physical backup media must be protected as well. For example, if I back up all my photos to an external storage device that is always plugged into the computer, the storage device might get encrypted if the computer is hit by ransomware. Fire, flood, earthquake, or simply a bottle of water that might spill over

Scams, Hacking, and Cybersecurity

the device could physically damage it and result in data loss. Therefore, I recommend keeping the backup copy in a safe place away from the main computer, otherwise it could get damaged by the same accident or disaster as the computer that holds the master copy.

Not everyone can afford to pay high monthly fees for a dedicated offsite backup service. However, one can always create an ad-hoc offsite backup by taking the backup media to the office or asking to keep it at a family member's or friend's house. Indeed, this approach requires discipline: remembering to bring the backup media home with you so you can back up the data and then return it for safekeeping. The risk vs. effort of this approach is something one has to consider as part of the personal risk management process.

What About a Recovery Test?

> **HOW CAN YOU FIX SOMETHING IF YOU DON'T KNOW WHAT'S BROKEN?**
> (OLIVIA BAKER, 13 REASONS WHY)

A backup is only as good as the ability to restore the data reliably. Remember the story about the photos of my mom that I couldn't open? A corrupt or inaccessible backup is useless in an emergency. Most companies have a strict backup strategy, and all the mission-critical data is backed up periodically. Some even contract an offsite backup company that sends a courier to collect the backup media and deliver it to a safe offsite backup location.

Scams, Hacking, and Cybersecurity

This was exactly what a New-York-based company had done. Once a week, a courier came, picked up the backup tapes, and delivered them to a remote site in the city for safekeeping. After a couple of years, the company office, including the server room, got flooded. Operations immediately leased and set up a temporary office while the IT team retrieved the backup tapes from the offsite backup location. It was the moment of truth. The IT team started to restore the data. First tape — corrupt data; second tape — corrupt data, and so on. It turned out that most of the tapes retrieved from the offsite backup locations were corrupt and practically useless. An investigation was launched and found that the couriers took the subway due to heavy traffic in the city center. The magnetic fields emitted from the subway's devices were strong enough to corrupt the data. It should be noted that current storage devices are far less susceptible to external influence, but if there's one thing history has taught us, is that you can never anticipate everything that could go wrong.

The company took backups regularly and even stored them safely offsite. However, the company failed to perform restoration testing and therefore didn't discover the problem on time, which would have allowed for the necessary adjustments to be made to ensure the backups were intact and accessible when needed.

> *A backup that cannot be restored is as good as useless.*

For those of us who backup our personal data to the cloud, it's recommended to periodically log into the cloud service and verify that all the backed-up data is there, and even to download a copy and verify that it works properly.

Scams, Hacking, and Cybersecurity

The number of transistors in a dense integrated circuit (IC) doubles about every two years
(Gordon Moore)

Moore's Law is a predication made in 1965 by Gordon Moore, the co-founder of Intel. Simply put, Moore predicted the progress rate of computing power. Moore observed that computing power doubles every 18-24 months with no changes to the manufacturing costs or microchip size. Indeed, for decades Moore's Law proved correct, as every new and shiny chip that was released became completely obsolete after merely two years.

Moore's Law resonated with me a couple of years ago while working as an information security consultant in a medium-sized financial services company.

The company followed all regulations, practices common sense and backed up the data to tapes shipped to an offsite location for safekeeping.

One day, one of the executives asked us to restore all his emails between specific dates six years earlier. The company was involved in a legal proceeding at the time, and the executive recalled an email correspondence that could potentially decide the legal dispute in the company's favor. He even remembered the quarter in which the correspondence took place.

The IT manager called the offsite backup company and asked for the relevant backup tapes.

The tapes arrived at our offices, and then we discovered a problem.

Scams, Hacking, and Cybersecurity

In technology, six years are an eternity. The backup tapes were based on an outdated technology and the company no longer had a tape drive that could read them.

> For those of us who might be less familiar with the backup world, the situation was similar to someone handing you over a CD with data on it. Do you have an optical disc drive at home?

Once again, no restoration testing was done and therefore the problem wasn't identified soon enough. If the company only realized that some of the backups were stored on the older tape format, they would have kept the tape drive or transferred all the backups to new and more current backup media.

For more details about backups, visit[22]:

---

[22] https://www.maybrooks.net/backups+

Scams, Hacking, and Cybersecurity

Protecting our kids[23]

Parents ask their children "where are you going" before they go out? They also ask them: "Who are you meeting?", "When will you be back?" and other similar questions. When they come back, we ask them "how was it?", "what did you do?", "who did you play with?" etc. But why don't we ask them those same questions when they're alone in their room on the computer?

Studies that looked at the impact of technology on family life found that parents who show interest and are involved in their children's digital world manage to significantly reduce their children's screen time and significantly increase the likelihood the children will share when they feel distressed.

A book about information security in the digital age would be incomplete without a chapter about children's online safety.

First and foremost, I want to stress that there's no absolute answer. The recommendations in this chapter are based on my professional opinion as a cybersecurity leader and not as an educator or psychologist.

Here are some statistics published in 2023 by the Israeli National Department for Children Online Protection - 105:

---

[23] Thanks to Amir Gefen, Ph.D. from the 105 Hotline of the Child Online Protection Bureau, and Orna Heilinger from the Israel Internet Association, who provided statistics and insights that helped me write this chapter.

Scams, Hacking, and Cybersecurity

In 2022, The Israeli National Department for Children Online Safety handled:

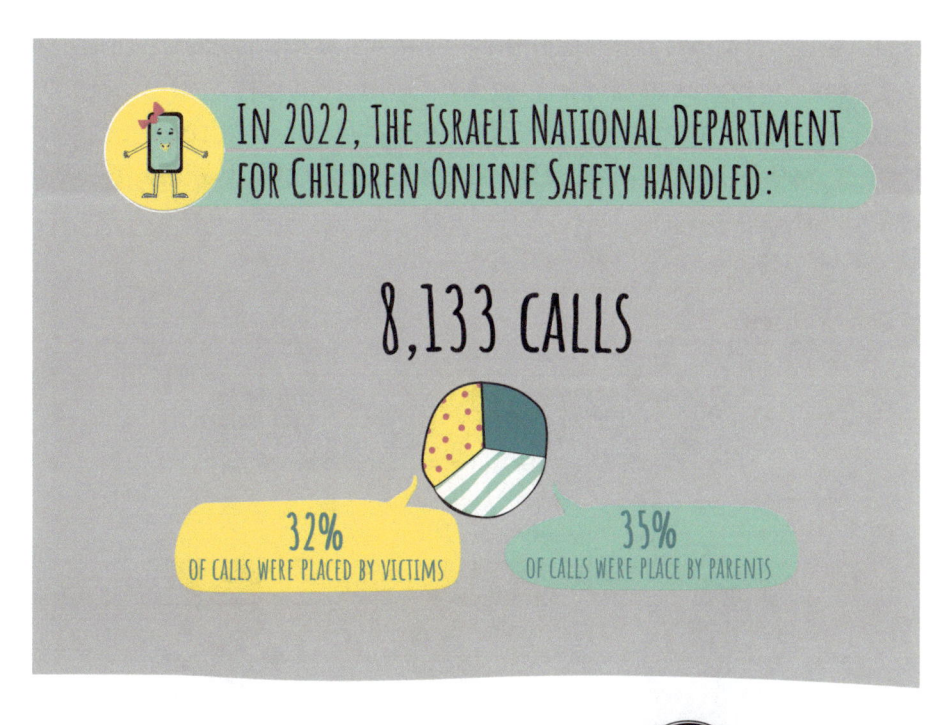

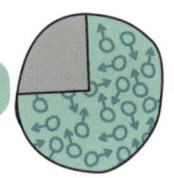

8,133 CALLS

32% OF CALLS WERE PLACED BY VICTIMS

35% OF CALLS WERE PLACE BY PARENTS

The average age of victims — 12

76% OF OFFENDERS ARE BOYS (UNDERAGED AND ADULTS)

67% OF VICTIMS ARE UNDERAGED GIRLS

64% OF OFFENDERS ARE UNDERAGED

31% BOYS AND TEENS

Scams, Hacking, and Cybersecurity

This chapter won't address the recommended screen time for children because I believe this is a parental decision that doesn't necessarily apply to safety, and I also believe that the decision should consider the type of online activity the children engage in. I will, however, explain how to protect children in the digital world of the 21st century.

The Dangers Children Face Online

WHAT CONCERNS PARENTS:

| Malware | Excessive Use (Addiction) | Explicit Content |
| Cyber Bullying | Sexual Harassment | Social Engineering |

- Inappropriate content: this is by far one of the most challenging problems in the internet era. In the past, people had to show a valid ID or a driver's license before they were allowed to

Scams, Hacking, and Cybersecurity

watch an R-rated movie in the theater, today, our children and we have virtually unlimited access to any type of content right at our fingertips. The age-restriction mechanisms of platforms such as YouTube are limited. Therefore, violent, and disturbing videos that are uploaded aren't always flagged at a timely manner, and as a result, young children are exposed to inappropriate content. Content also flows on direct messaging apps without control, thus exposing kids.

> *YouTube, Instagram, TikTok, and other social media platforms restrict children under the age of 13 from using their services.*

- Online sexual abuse: online sexual abuse is probably one of the topics that worry parents most, and rightfully so. Online anonymity enables direct communication. Messages sent from unknown numbers on WhatsApp are quite common. Inappropriate messages from known and unknown senders, can expose our children to explicit content including texts, pictures, and links.

- Social Engineering: children and adolescents are often targeted by social engineers. In some cases, they're targeted for financial benefits, like convincing them to order something online or provide their parents credit card number. In other cases, the attack is more targeted. Law enforcement agencies around the world are fighting against online sexual grooming, in which child molesters build an online relationship with their potential target. This relationship can lead to online or real-world abuse. Those attackers use the same social engineering principles described previously in the book.

Scams, Hacking, and Cybersecurity

- Excessive use (addiction): in late 2018, the media reported an addiction to the Fortnite video game among adolescents. It became so severe that some adolescents needed rehab. Fortnite, however, isn't the first addictive video game, nor the last. There were similar concerns in the 90s regarding video games such as Doom and Pac-Man. When a video game is available on a computer, tablet, or smartphone, the potential for an addiction is even greater. It's important to note that too much screen time doesn't necessarily point to an addiction. Addiction is a disorder that can only be diagnosed by a healthcare professional, but any unreasonable use that results in loss of interest in social activities, skipping school, and hurts other life aspects, could be deemed excessive use.

- Dangerous challenges: kids of the 90s probably remember the sour candy dare challenge, the black candy (the sourest!) was my favorite. Dare challenges are not new, and like everything else in our digital world they've moved on to the realm of social media. Recent reports show an increase in the number of online dare challenges targeting children and adolescents. In 2016 a new challenge made headlines: the Blue Whale Challenge. The players were assigned tasks they had to complete over a 50-day period. If they failed to do so, they were told their personal details would be published online. The tasks involved self-harm, such as self-scarring, sleep deprivation, and watching horror films. The last challenge allegedly required the players to jump from the tallest building they could find and practically commit suicide. Though some claim the Blue Whale challenge was made up, copycats soon followed and similar, real challenges were created. In 2018, a new challenge called the 'Momo Challenge' got public attention. Momo was the fictional character allegedly sending the messages. The ghastly image of a goggle-eyed

Scams, Hacking, and Cybersecurity

creature with black hair and a terrifying face that was based on a sculpture by a Japanese artist[24].

The challenge spread quickly because every new player was asked to add another friend to the game. The administrators used data they collected on the players and sent threats and scary photos to entice the players to perform a series of dangerous tasks, including self-harm. Momo's terrifying photo and the threats caused panic among children and adolescents, and are linked to several suicide attempts.

In late 2019, TikTok became the popular platform for challenges. Some challenges and trends, such as dance challenges that swept teenagers all over the world, were harmless. However, others were dangerous and included jumping from rooftops, inhaling refrigerant gas, holding one's breath, and a dance where one of the dancers gets tripped over and falls on their head.

- Cyberbullying: children can be cruel; this has always been the case. That said, social media has taken bullying to new levels. Abusive messages sent anonymously, cyber shaming, and shuns on WhatsApp groups without the teachers' knowledge. If in the past moving to another school was deemed a good solution in some cases, today things are considerably different. The idea of a new start becomes moot when the new classmates of the victim can dig up what happened in the old school in a click of a button. There's a domestic and global effort to raise awareness and minimize this phenomenon, but cyberbullying remains a main online dangers for children and adolescents and had led to several suicide attempts.

---

[24] If you want to see the original sculpture Momo was based on, please click here: https://www.japantimes.co.jp/news/2019/03/06/national/social-issues/japanese-artist-behind-ghastly-creature-viral-momo-challenge-baffled-disturbing-hoax/#.XojiOYgzaUk

Scams, Hacking, and Cybersecurity

Treat others the way you want to be treated.

This sentence, comes to my mind every time I come across a rude comment or a story about cyberbullying. As people transition from personal interaction to impersonal digital interactions, they seem to feel freer to be rude, mean, and say things they would have never said to someone face to face. It's easy to forget that there's a real person with real feelings on the other side. This is true for children and adults, who engage and experience cyberbullying as well.

- Malware: the same cybersecurity threats to adults' computers and mobile devices apply to children and adolescents' devices and online activity. Phishing attacks, virus, ransomware, and other types of malwares do not know nor care about the age of the potential victims.

Protecting Children Online:

Every parent wants to protect their children. Nowadays, there's a wide variety of parental control solutions, from basic freeware to complex systems that not only monitor the child's online activity but also analyze their mood and mental state based on their communications and search history.

Each parent knows what they're comfortable with and where to draw the line. Before we allow our children to use a mobile device, we must lay out some ground rules.

Some families restrict how long or where a child is allowed to use a mobile device. Other parents ask to review everything their

Scams, Hacking, and Cybersecurity

children do on their phone, or use automatic monitoring tools.

There are two main types of parental control:

1. Content filtering
2. Parental monitoring applications

Content Filtering:

As explained earlier in this chapter, exposure to inappropriate content is one of the biggest concerns for parents. Adults exercise discretion and avoid exposure to content they find inappropriate. But how can we protect children from inappropriate content, especially when they do not fully understand the ramifications of being exposed to such content.

Internet Service Provider (ISP) and phone carries offer a variety of free and paid content filtering solutions. In some countries, the service providers are mandated by law to offer website and inappropriate content filtering (porn, violence, and gambling) free of charge as part of their license.

> *Contact your ISP or phone carrier and make sure content filtering is turned on for your children.*

One caveat is that the content filtering will only work when the child's device is connected to the home Wi-Fi network or uses the data plan. What should you do if your child might connect to other networks too?

Scams, Hacking, and Cybersecurity

Well, there are two solutions here: having a candid and honest conversation with your child about online safety, and installing a content filtering application on their device. These solutions should be used together, it's not a case of one or the other.

Parental Monitoring and Control Tools

Some parental monitoring applications claim to be able to detect inappropriate, offensive, or abusive words and even the child's mood, which could alert the parents in case the child is in any kind of distress. However, it's important to remember:

> *Technological measures are not a substitute for having an open and candid conversation about online safety.*

We have a limited ability to control the content that our children are exposed to. You can monitor and read every message your child receives, but should you?

Technically speaking, as parents we have the right to install cameras in our children's rooms and watch every move they make. Yet, most people don't do that. Children have a right to privacy[25]. Installing a monitoring application is akin to installing a camera and should be done after a discussion with the child, specifying what is being monitored and the family rules for screen time and internet use. It's our responsibility as parents to equip our children with tools that will allow them to avoid the pitfalls of misinforms and online distortion of reality, as well as discuss online dangers.

---

[25] With the exception of cases where close monitoring is required due to past incidents.

Scams, Hacking, and Cybersecurity

A Thought Exercise:

Would you help your children obtain a fake ID to buy alcoholic beverages before they reached the legal drinking age?

I assume the answer to this question is an overwhelming no. Similarly, when you help your children create their first email account and fake their age to 13, because they really want to use apps like TikTok, Instagram, and YouTube, you're not helping them; you're exposing them to danger. The age restrictions are there for several reasons, including limited content filtering capabilities and child privacy protection laws[26]. When a user profile claims that the user is 15, they will see content that was liked by other 15 YO, the same is true is the profile is set to 33. When you create a child account that does not reflect their age, or if you let your children use your device, they will see content that is not age appropriate for them, because as far as the platforms are concerned – the set user age is the deciding factor.

> *Want to protect your children? Don't help them fake their age online.*

Setting Ground Rules:

As I've mentioned at the beginning of this chapter, different families have different rules for screen time and internet use. In some families, mobile devices are forbidden at the table or during family time, other families restrict the number of hours their child may use a mobile device, and in some families, there are no restrictions at all.

---

[26] For example, the United States federal law Children's Online Privacy Protection Act ("COPPA")

Scams, Hacking, and Cybersecurity

I recommend putting down some ground rules, an agreement between parents and children, before your children get their first mobile device. Of course, those ground rules can and should be adjusted over time.

You can download a free sample of the Smartphone Usage Agreement here[27]:

[QR code]

All the information in this book applies to children as well. It's our responsibility as parents to convey this information to our children:

---

[27] https://maybrooks.net/Kids.html

Scams, Hacking, and Cybersecurity

- **THINK BEFORE TAKING OR SHARING A PHOTO**

- **THERE ARE REAL PEOPLE WITH REAL EMOTIONS ON THE OTHER SIDE**

- **LOOK FOR ONLINE THREATS WARNING SIGNS**

- **AVOID OVERSHARING ON SOCIAL MEDIA (UPDATE YOUR PRIVACY SETTINGS)**

- **BACKUP DATA (IT'S NEVER TOO YOUNG TO START)**

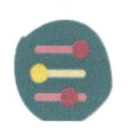

- **TEACH THEM GOOD PASSWORD PRACTICES**

I'm a strong believer that a candid open dialogue and teaching children online safety practices are the key to a safer world.

If you want to learn more about keeping your kids safe online, checkout my CyberWise Parenting[28] course. This concise and practical course will give you all the tools you need to protect your child online, now and in the future.

Scams, Hacking, and Cybersecurity

What About Privacy?

Anything you've ever searched online, any website you've visited, places you've been, every voice command you gave Siri or Alexa are logged and recorded. This is the Information Age in a nutshell. Have you ever googled something only to discover later that all your ads were related to that item or subject? It's no coincidence and your mind isn't playing tricks on you. It's called targeted advertising. Targeted ads directly benefit consumers by displaying relevant ads for things they're actually interested in. If you're looking for a new car, you'll see car ads; if you're researching your next vacation in Japan, you'll see ads for hotels and activities that might help you plan your trip. The disadvantage is selective exposure. I might already know which car I want, but being exposed to targeted advertising might lead me to choose a different car. Did I choose correctly? Only time will tell.

No, Google and Facebook do not actively "listen" to your conversations, they don't have to. They already know not only what you're interested in, but also what your friends and family members are interested in. If a few of my online friends 'liked' a specific ad, or even went ahead and purchased something, it stands to reason the same ad will be relevant to me. That's digital age marketing, or, in its professional term "behavior engineering".

[28] https://maybrooks.net/CyberWiseParenting.html

Targeted advertising raises privacy concerns, and experts predict that as the world becomes more tech-driven, we'll lose even more of our privacy. Soon, we'll all wear smart glasses that will show us ads based on our environment. Imagine kicking back on the sofa, when suddenly an ad pops up for a carpet that really brightens up the room.

The perception of privacy is changing before our very eyes, and so does correlating legislation. The General Data Protection Regulation (GDPR) that was introduced by the EU in 2018 raised the bar in several essential aspects, including:

- The right to be forgotten: every time you use the internet you leave a digital trail behind: your search history, messages you've sent, pictures you've shared, and websites you've visited. GDPR allows individuals to ask organizations to delete their personal data held in the organization's database. As of writing these lines, this right applies only to EU citizens.

- Fines: the EU may issue fines up to €20M or up to 4%, whichever is greater, for GDPR violations.

The European legislation is considered extremely strict and had been the subject of numerous lawsuits against global companies who didn't appear to adhere to it. In 2023, Threads app was launched by Meta (Facebook) in over one hundred countries including the US and the UK, however the app was restricted for EU users (as of July 2023).

Privacy is a complicated subject. I claim that privacy doesn't really exist in the 21st century. The details of my location, who I speak with, with who I meet, what I search for, and where I plan to go on my next vacation are stored somewhere in digital files that I cannot control. I don't know with whom this information is shared and for what purpose.

Scams, Hacking, and Cybersecurity

I originally wrote this chapter in late March 2020, amid the global COVID-19 pandemic. During the pandemic, several countries required citizens to install a health monitoring app on their phones. Some countries approved tracking of suspected and confirmed COVID-19 patients. The technology had allowed for mass surveillance aimed at controlling the spread of the virus, but at what cost? Are we okay with our government tracking our every move?

A key difference between Google knowing everything about me and my government knowing everything about me, is that Google doesn't have the power to arrest or penalize me.

We're living in interesting times. Is saving lives more important than someone's privacy? Who will determine where the surveillance had gone too far?

Some privacy aspects are still up to us. Exercise good judgement and common sense. Some things are better kept private. There's no need to post any random thought that crosses your mind. Your current location isn't necessarily everyone's business. Not all photos should be shared with others, or even taken for that matter. Always remember:

> *The internet is like an Elephant - it never forgets.*

This book has thoroughly discussed the risks of oversharing on social media and the privacy concerns over tracking our browsing and search history, location data, and more.

In recent years, microchip parties became quite the trend in

Sweden. Thousands of people, and sometimes entire families, come to these parties and get an under-skin microchip implanted. Each chip contains a unique ID number linked to identifiable information and replaces their credit card, keys, access cards, and can be used for other applications. The microchip uses Near Field Communication (NFC) technology, similar to the embedded chip used in contactless credit cards. Early adopters of this technology maintain that this is the future. The chip makes life more convenient, gone are the days of searching for your wallet or car keys. It even has a health benefit. When an unconscious person arrives at the hospital, the medical team can scan the implant and access the patient's medical records. Microchip and implant owners believe this is only the first step and that we'll all get implanted with multiple microchips that will improve our quality of life in the future.

Critiques, on the other hand, warn us about the end of privacy and say it's only a matter of time before these systems and databases get hacked.

These debates are always about the very delicate, and sometimes elusive, sweet spot between privacy and convenience. Which school of thought will be proven right? Only time will tell.

Privacy Settings

When I first started to think about writing this book, I also started to save posts from Facebook, labeling them "things that should have never been posted". Confessions of infidelity, asking for advice about health or medical conditions, people posting from the beach while telling their boss they're sick etc. Many of these posts were originally published on supposedly closed groups. Why do I say supposedly? Because while one can't share content posted to a closed group with people outside the group, nothing

Scams, Hacking, and Cybersecurity

stops users from copying entire messages or sharing screenshots. This is true not only to closed groups on Facebook — we already covered the risks of oversharing on social media — but also to one's personal Facebook page, Instagram posts, and questions we send on WhatsApp groups.

One post that really resonated with me, was that of a worried mother, her 8 YO child was still wetting his bed. She shared her concerns in a public Facebook group. My issue with this post wasn't the content, it was the fact that this post could be found in the future by this child's classmates, and as mentioned before, kids can be cruel.

Lately Facebook added the "post anonymously" option in many of its online groups and communities. While some people just started posting everything anonymously, reducing personal involvement, others use it to post things they are uncomfortable having traced back to them, and that is a great step in the right direction!

The first and most important rule on social media is to exercise good judgement and use common sense. The internet doesn't forget and everything you publish might come back to haunt you in the future. A compromising photo you uploaded at 17, a meme you shared when you were angry with your supervisor, or a rude or blatant comment you made after reading an article – are all there for prosperity, and like it or not, this is the type of content that tends to attract unwanted attention.

Scams, Hacking, and Cybersecurity

In addition to using good judgement, you should adjust the privacy settings on all your social media accounts.

I recommend disabling Location Services on all your social media apps. It's unnecessary and exposes you to a greater risk. Note: parental monitoring solutions aren't affected by these settings and you will still be able to track the location of your child's device.

For more details about privacy and privacy settings, visit[29]:

[29] https://www.maybrooks.net/privacy

Predicting the Future

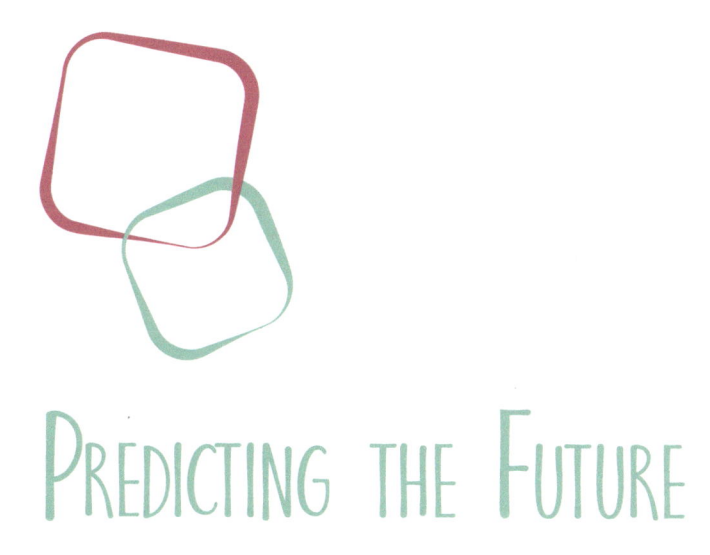

At the beginning of this book, I mentioned that on October 29, 1969 the first message was sent through the ARPANET network, which eventually evolved into the Internet. Over the 5 decades since, and more notably in the past 2 decades, the internet has changed our everyday lives. It transformed entire industries. Gone are the days of having to meet with a travel agent to book a flight. Today, booking a flight is as easy as opening an app on your phone. Will the continued evolution of Augmented Reality and Virtual Reality technologies replace traditional travel? Will a virtual tour of the Sistine Chapel, immediately followed by watching a stunning sunset on a virtual Thai beach be enough?

Smart watches, security systems, smart homes, and pacemakers are already part of the Internet of Things (IoT), and as technology continues to improve, the number of connected devices, objects, and appliances will only increase. Self-driving cars are predicted to disrupt and transform the auto industry. Artificial Intelligence allows us to create content like never before. Cryptocurrency is

Scams, Hacking, and Cybersecurity

gaining a widespread acceptance and the demise of cash and flat currency seems inevitable.

> ## CRIMINALS USUALLY PREY ON WEAKNESS. THEY CAN SMELL IT.
> ### (STEVEN SEAGAL)

Over the years the internet protocol was heavily criticized for its flaws. Many have questioned why it wasn't designed to be more secure in the first place. The answer is simple: back then no one considered the threat of cybercriminals. They didn't exist. None of the researchers in that UCLA lab back in the 60s ever envisioned how this new communication protocol would transform the world, for better and worse, for decades to come.

There are estimations that the number of implanted connected medical devices will increase significantly in the coming years. Self-driving cars are already a reality. Smart goggles are in active development. You cannot, and should not, escape the internet, but you can use it safely.

The use of the internet and social media is not going to decrease. Younger generations don't have the luxury of putting their past behind them. The digital world never forgets. Anyone can find and look at your past. We must remember that people change and their deeds as teens don't necessarily reflect who they are in their 20s, 30s, 40s and so on. This change in mindset can help us handle incidents such as Sextortion and revenge porn, that could potentially ruin people's lives.

Scams, Hacking, and Cybersecurity

I believe that new innovative tools will change our lives for the better and help us use personal and global resources more efficiently. However, as we become more reliant on the internet, there will be those who will look to abuse these tools. The more devices, objects, and appliances we connect to the web, the more cyber-attacks will occur.

How will the Information Security field respond to these changes? Well, I believe that some of the tools I described in this book will remain relevant, others less so, but the basic online safety principles and guidelines will always be true.

- Think before you share.
- Think before you click.
- Think ahead and protect.

Think Safe — Stay Safe

And... Don't click here :)

Glossary

- RAM (Random Access Memory): a form of internal memory that can be read and changed in any order. The RAM holds the information of the applications installed on the device, your contacts list, and other data.

- ROM (Read Only Memory): a computer's permanent memory. It cannot be modified and retains the stored information even after power is removed (non-volatile memory). This memory stores the operating system of the computer or smartphone. The user cannot change the information stored on the ROM. The device manufacturer writes the data to the ROM during the manufacturing process and it cannot be changed again, making it a read-only memory.

- Processing power: determines how many tasks the computer can execute simultaneously. The available processing power depends on the type of processor, its frequency, and other parameters.

- The CIA triad (Confidentiality, Integrity, Availability): an Information Security model consisting three key concepts:

    * **Confidentiality:** protecting the information from unauthorized access.

    * **Integrity:** maintaining and assuring the accuracy and completeness of data.

    * **Availability:** ensuring the information is available when it is needed.

Scams, Hacking, and Cybersecurity

- **Darknet:** a hidden network on the internet that is inaccessible through regular search engines and can only be accessed using a special browser. The darknet is anonymous and therefore used for illegal activities, such as selling through dedicated markets, drugs, ransomware, cyber-arms, hacking services, pornographic content, illicit activity within organizations (whistle-blowing), and even murderer-for-hire.

- **Vulnerability:** a weakness which can be exploited by an attacker.

- **Malware (malicious software):** any software designed to cause damage to a computer, device, or a computer network. Malware is a generic name for a wide variety of malicious software, including computer viruses, ransomware, and Trojan horses.

- **Zero-day (also known as 0-day):** a software vulnerability unknown to the vendor. Zero-day vulnerabilities are popular with hackers because they allow them to execute targeted attacks that go unnoticed by security systems.

- **Ransomware:** a malicious computer program that encrypts all the user files and then demands a ransom payment to decrypt them.

- **Phishing:** a type of social engineering attack designed to trick the user into revealing sensitive information or deploy malicious software.

- **Vishing (voice phishing):** a phishing attack carried out over the phone. Vishing scammers typically pose as an employee of a legitime body such as the bank or a credit card company.

- **Smishing (SMS phishing):** a phishing attack carried out over text messages. This type of attack has been recently on the rise, also because it's more difficult to detect malicious links in a text message and altering the sender identification is easy.

- **Spear phishing:** a phishing attack targeting a specific individual, organization or business, sometimes only as a means to get to someone else who's the real target.
- **Embedded system:** any device with a dedicated combination of computer hardware and software designed to perform a specific function.
- **Sextortion:** a type of online blackmail where the victim is threatened that their intimate photos will be shared with others unless certain demands are met.
- **Plaintext:** the unencrypted data one wants to encrypt.
- **Cyphertext:** the plaintext data after it was encrypted. Cyphertext cannot be read without a decryption key.
- **Encryption:** the process of converting plain-text or data into cipher-text
- **Decryption:** the process of converting cyphertext into its original plaintext form.
- **Symmetric encryption:** using the same key for encrypting and decrypting the data.
- **Asymmetric encryption:** using a pair of related keys — one public and the other private — to encrypt and decrypt data.

Scams, Hacking, and Cybersecurity

- **Hash function:** a one-way function — a function which is practically infeasible to invert or reverse — used primarily to verify that the data hasn't changed.

- **Multi-factor authentication (MFA, also two-factor authentication or 2FA):** the use of at least two of the three following factors for authentication:

    » Something you know (a password or PIN)

    » Something you have (a physical object such as a security token or phone)

    » Something you are (biometrics)

REFERENCES

(in alphabetical order)

http://practicalcryptography.com/

http://raidxstorage.bandilabs.com/2017/01/04/cost-per-gigabyte/

http://raidxstorage.bandilabs.com/2017/01/04/cost-per-gigabyte/

https://9to5google.com/2019/10/02/google-password-checkup-chrome/

https://computer.howstuffworks.com/future-of-the-internet.htm

https://computing.which.co.uk/hc/en-gb/articles/360001317945-How-to-respond-to-a-sextortion-email

https://computing.which.co.uk/hc/en-gb/articles/360001317945-How-to-respond-to-a-sextortion-email

https://cybersecurityventures.com/global-ransomware-damage-costs-predicted-to-reach-20-billion-usd-by-2021/

https://cybersecurityventures.com/global-ransomware-damage-costs-predicted-to-reach-20-billion-usd-by-2021/

https://darknetdiaries.com/

https://docs.broadcom.com/doc/istr-24-2019-en

https://en.wikipedia.org/wiki/Andrew_Fastow

https://en.wikipedia.org/wiki/Arthur_Andersen

https://en.wikipedia.org/wiki/Cryptography#Computer_era

https://en.wikipedia.org/wiki/Enron#2001_Accounting_scandals

https://en.wikipedia.org/wiki/Jeffrey_Skilling

https://en.wikipedia.org/wiki/Kenneth_Lay

Scams, Hacking, and Cybersecurity

https://en.wikipedia.org/wiki/Lorenz_cipher

https://en.wikipedia.org/wiki/Revenge_porn

https://en.wikipedia.org/wiki/Sarbanes%E2%80%93Oxley_Act

https://en.wikipedia.org/wiki/WannaCry_ransomware_attack

https://gizmodo.com/its-time-to-nervously-mock-the-50-worst-passwords-of-th-1840514905

https://haveibeenpwned.com/

https://he.wikipedia.org/wiki/%D7%94%D7%9E%D7%A2%D7%99%D7%9C%D7%94_%D7%91%D7%91%D7%A0%D7%A7_%D7%9C%D7%9E%D7%A1%D7%97%D7%A8

https://he.wikipedia.org/wiki/%D7%9C%D7%95%D7%95%D7%99%D7%99%D7%AA%D7%9F_%D7%9B%D7%97%D7%95%D7%9C_(%D7%9E%D7%A9%D7%97%D7%A7)

https://pdf.ic3.gov/2018_IC3Report.pdf

https://resources.infosecinstitute.com/password-security-complexity-vs-length/#gref

https://storage.googleapis.com/gweb-uniblog-publish-prod/documents/PasswordCheckup-HarrisPoll-InfographicFINAL.pdf

https://storage.googleapis.com/gweb-uniblog-publish-prod/documents/PasswordCheckup-HarrisPoll-InfographicFINAL.pdf

https://tech.walla.co.il/item/3137364

https://unctad.org/en/pages/PublicationWebflyer.aspx?publicationid=2466

https://www.2-remove-virus.com/sextortion-email-scams-on-the-rise/

https://www.2-remove-virus.com/sextortion-email-scams-on-the-rise/

https://www.accenture.com/_acnmedia/pdf-96/accenture-2019-cost-of-cybercrime-study-final.pdf

Scams, Hacking, and Cybersecurity

https://www.boi.org.il/he/BankingSupervision/SupervisorsDirectives/DocLib/357.pdf

https://www.calcalist.co.il/local/articles/0,7340,L-3801811,00.html

https://www.carbonblack.com/wp-content/uploads/2016/09/Ransomware_Timeline_Carbon_Black.jpg

https://www.cnet.com/how-to/new-years-resolution-protect-your-credentials-with-the-google-chrome-password-manager/

https://www.cosmopolitan.com/sex-love/advice/a30675/ninety-percent-millennial-women-take-nude-photos-cosmo-survey/

https://www.enigmasoftware.com/top-5-popular-cybercrimes-how-easily-prevent-them/

https://www.forbes.com/2003/09/04/0904bookreview.html#4bc81b164f64

https://www.forbes.com/sites/leemathews/2017/08/16/notpetya-ransomware-attack-cost-shipping-giant-maersk-over-200-million/#2d8b31734f9a

https://www.forcepoint.com/blog/insights/the-future-of-cybersecurity-proactive-predictive-dynamic

https://www.gartner.com/en/newsroom/press-releases/2018-08-15-gartner-forecasts-worldwide-information-security-spending-to-exceed-124-billion-in-2019

https://www.globes.co.il/news/article.aspx?did=1000968439

https://www.gov.il/he/departments/publications/reports/minors_in_cyberspace_issue_2

https://www.gov.il/he/departments/Units/105_call_center

https://www.gsmarena.com/apple_iphone_11-9848.php

https://www.gsmarena.com/apple_iphone_11-9848.php

https://www.haaretz.co.il/misc/1.1203494

Scams, Hacking, and Cybersecurity

https://www.inc.com/jason-aten/google-says-66-of-americans-still-do-this-1-thing-that-puts-their-personal-information-at-a-huge-risk-heres-how-google-wants-to-help.html

https://www.inc.com/jason-aten/google-says-66-of-americans-still-do-this-1-thing-that-puts-their-personal-information-at-a-huge-risk-heres-how-google-wants-to-help.html

https://www.internetsociety.org/blog/2019/07/internet-societys-online-trust-alliance-2019-cyber-incidents-breach-trends-report/?gclid=Cj0KCQjw6_vzBRCIARIsAOs54z6TcK2o9ECEveR7dzypKnNiEDLIuBIgjcsd6UBAcnpRL70Wvu1xvOMaAum2EALw_wcB

https://www.israelhayom.co.il/article/731797

https://www.kaspersky.com/resource-center/threats/ransomware-wannacry

https://www.link11.com/en/blog/infographic-here-are-10-reasons-why-cyber-security-needs-to-be-top-priority-in-2019/

https://www.link11.com/en/blog/infographic-here-are-10-reasons-why-cyber-security-needs-to-be-top-priority-in-2019/

https://www.mako.co.il/entertainment-celebs/world/Article-c40f6d126ff2841006.htm

https://www.malwarefox.com/ransomware-statistics-infographic/

https://www.pc.co.il/featured/274226/

https://www.pcmag.com/picks/the-best-free-password-managers

https://www.pcmag.com/picks/the-best-password-managers

https://www.popularmechanics.com/technology/infrastructure/a29666802/future-of-the-internet/

https://www.science20.com/the_conversation/is_your_cell_phone_more_powerful_than_nasas_apollo_guidance_computer-239388

https://www.science20.com/the_conversation/is_your_cell_phone_more_powerful_than_nasas_apollo_guidance_computer-239388

https://www.space.com/11700-nasa-computer-hacked-satellite-data-

Scams, Hacking, and Cybersecurity

tinkode.html

https://www.technotification.com/2019/04/ncsc-worlds-most-hacked-passwords.html/

https://www.thesslstore.com/blog/20-phishing-statistics-to-keep-you-from-getting-hooked-in-2019/

https://www.theverge.com/2011/10/31/2526480/us-satellites-attacked-hackers-chinese-military-nasa

https://www.varonis.com/blog/cybersecurity-statistics/

https://www.washingtonpost.com/news/the-fix/wp/2015/08/26/6-cases-where-the-ashley-madison-leak-has-ensnared-political-and-public-officials/

https://www.washingtonpost.com/news/the-fix/wp/2015/08/26/6-cases-where-the-ashley-madison-leak-has-ensnared-political-and-public-officials/

https://www.weforum.org/agenda/2019/09/4-ways-ai-is-changing-cybersecurity-both-in-attack-and-defense/

https://www.weforum.org/agenda/2019/11/cost-cybercrime-cybersecurity/

https://www.wired.com/story/notpetya-cyberattack-ukraine-russia-code-crashed-the-world/

https://www.ynet.co.il/articles/0,7340,L-5340992,00.html

https://www.youtube.com/watch?v=e5qC1YGRMKI

https://www.youtube.com/watch?v=hwollZoVmUc

https://www.youtube.com/watch?v=rDyMz1V-GSg

https://www.zdnet.com/article/maersk-forced-to-reinstall-4000-servers-45000-pcs-due-to-notpetya-attack/

CREDITS:

I was entertaining the idea of writing this book for a long while, and this dream wouldn't have been made possible without the support of some dear people, whom I want to use this opportunity to thank:

Itamar – my second half, the man who always knows what to say (and what not to say). Thank you for who you are, for who we are, for your love and for believing no mountain is too high. Your faith in me makes me believe in myself.

Shiri, Yuval, and Naomi Ziv – this book wouldn't have been possible without you. Thank you for your inspiration, hugs, curious questions, and the laughter, I'm in this business to make this world a safer place for you!

Dad – for asking about this book every time we met for our morning walk, for the encouragement and support I always received from you and **Mum**. Thank you for teaching me that anything is possible, for believing in me, and for always having my back.

Matan — my dear little big brother! Thank you for reading, critiquing, encouraging, pushing, supporting, making me laugh, sharing, and for always being there for me.

Bat-Hen – thank you for your clear thinking, focus and organization skills that always leave me in awe, your support, ideas, and above all, your friendship.

Scams, Hacking, and Cybersecurity

Michal Nemtzov – a super-designer who immediately understood what I was looking for and turned my ideas into vivid graphics.

Yuval Abramovich, for your guidance, support, and inspiration. I could have never done any of it without you!

The closed-circuit:

People I can always trust to cheer me up when I'm feeling down, help me think outside the box, and always be there, through the good, bad, and ugly.

Thank you for your support and patience throughout this emotional rollercoaster of a project.

Avital Rappaport, Aviad Ravé, Orly Zamir, Itzik Zilberberg, Galia Ariav (and Udi, Ya'ara, Sivan, and Coony!)**, Hillel Kobrovesky, Channa Admanit Ganot, Luba Leor, Meidad Pariente, Nir Amkayess, Noa Gilboa, Adi Maor Siso, Einat Yarom Reich, Keren Shahar-Nissan, Ronen Hershkovitz, Rotem Golan, Rami Weiss, Shahar Cohen, Shelly Kotler, Ayelet Kamintz, Itay Gurovich, Bat-hen Zelig Gilad, Haim Malul, Natalia Sade, Anat Eylon, and Tom Malka.**

A special thanks also goes out to: Meital Bar Zohar, Gil Perez, Michael Dahan, Ran Bar-Zik, Amir Geffen, Itay Klein, Israel Schur, Omna Berick-Aharony, Tzvika Zelinger, Einat Lahav, Nadav Nachmias, and many others — thank you!